Rugs and Wall Hangings

Books by Maggie Lane

Needlepoint by Design
More Needlepoint by Design
Chinese Rugs Designed for Needlepoint

Rugs and Wall Hangings

Photographs by R. Lans Christensen

Maggie Lane

Charles Scribner's Sons   New York

TO
Mina and Louise

Copyright © 1976 Maggie Lane

Library of Congress Cataloging in Publication Data

Lane, Maggie.
    Rugs and wall hangings.

    Continues the author's Chinese rugs designed for
needlepoint.
    Bibliography: p. 161
    1. Rugs. 2. Wall hangings. I. Title.
TT850.L3   746.4′4   76-10177
ISBN 0-684-14670-3

Picture of a p'i p'a is reproduced by permission of
Charles E. Tuttle Co., Inc.

1 3 5 7 9 11 13 15 17 19 MD/C 20 18 16 14 12 10 8 6 4 2

Printed in the United States of America

Acknowledgments

I am indebted to many people for their contributions to this book.

To Lois Cowles, Louise de Paoli, Paul Griffith, June Shankland Hilliker, Barbara Brown Rubinstein, and Robert G. Taylor for making rugs and panels for this volume, and for finishing some of those I had already started—

To Charles Blackburn for blocking almost every one of the sample pieces—

To R. Lans Christensen for his enthusiasm and for his crisp, clear photographs—

To my husband for his patience and understanding when, due to overflowing wastebaskets and proliferating graphs, diagrams, canvases, and hanks of wool, our home from time to time almost burst its seams—

To Mary Mingione for checking the numbers of every Paternayan color used in the rugs and panels—

To Pat Smythe and Janet Hornberger for their artist's eye and meticulous care in the book's production—

And to Elinor Parker for her invaluable help in editing this book—

To every one of you I give my warmest thanks.

Contents

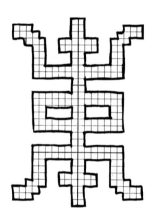

Foreword

The appearance of a fourth volume of Maggie Lane's needle-point designs calls more for a celebration than an introduction, so wide is her following by now and so substantial her achievement. Were this volume to be no more than a repetition of what she has already given us, no one would complain. But those who have followed Maggie Lane through each of her volumes have doubtless already noted that, together, her books reflect an unfolding awareness of the possibilities of needlepoint not only in the design of such conventional objects as pillows or hand-bags, where the field of design remains relatively small, but also in the creation of larger, less obviously functional pieces where problems of composition and execution are both more complex and more challenging. With this volume, Maggie Lane extends even further our appreciation of what can be done through needlepoint when the designer is also an artist.

Viewed from one perspective, a work of art is always a "borrowing." Its creator has depended both consciously and unconsciously on all that went before. Yet from another perspective, the artist's work is unique, the result of countless individual debates and decisions (including decisions to borrow this and not that) which combine in remarkable ways to give us one world—the world that the artist's eye has perceived as beautiful.

Let me suggest something of the process whereby an artist lays claim to an inherited world by recounting but a few of the decisions and choices that went into the making of one of the five panels to be found in this volume—the delightful dragon panel (pages 80–81). The work "began" one day when Maggie

ix

Lane happened to notice a scene on an embroidered hanging—a procession of children with sticks holding up the body of a paper dragon. Something about the gaiety of the scene caught her imagination, and although everything in this procession but the dragon himself was to be missing from *her* design, the mood of the happy children remained central to her conception of the panel.

Once removed from his original setting, the dragon changed his colors, taking on the lovely celadon that dominates the central field of the panel. And instead of festive children, he was finally to be accompanied by butterflies. This decision was the result of several transformations: another dragon scene, this time on a jardinière that appeared in a cosmetic ad, suggested the idea of stylized clouds as a background, but before these were realized, a cloud of elegant butterflies on an embroidered robe suggested another solution, with the result that instead of clouds we have seven blue, amethyst, and celadon butterflies caught up in the billow of the dragon. All that remains of the jardinière is the fine fretwork at the top of the panel.

But the butterflies raised new questions about color and position. Should all the butterflies dart above the waves of the dragon's rind? Only after many tries did the "right" positions reveal themselves. At one point a white butterfly was poised at the lower left of the dragon, facing him in order to stop the gay procession from moving right off the canvas! Later, the white was changed to blue to provide a more subtle halt.

There remained the problem of borders and bands. How was this lively dragon to be subdued before the viewer's eye reached the limits of the canvas? A sudden harsh line would not do; something peaceful yet powerful had to enclose the scene. The resolution appeared to come with the formal waves that roll across the base, and below them, the more severe band of pebbled white which forms a final base for all the activity above. Still, the waves were too sharply separated from blue sky until the idea of the three dots served to join sky and sea. Above, as if to balance the seven clusters of sea dots, seven stylized Chinese characters were superimposed upon the fretwork from the jardinière.

Like all successful performances, the completed piece, so ambitious in scale and so perfect in its mood of airy fantasy, bears no trace of this history. Yet were we to reconstruct the creation of every design in this volume we would find in each panel or rug a similar intricate history of decisions, each of which in some way altered the artist's conception of her design and at the same time served to reinforce her original version. We would find the same fortuitous discoveries of theme or feature in a range of sources, from cosmetic ads or musical instruments to temple rugs, and the same underlying persuasions about what is beautiful and worth laboring over to create.

For the reader who chooses to follow exactly the designs Maggie Lane has developed for this volume, there may be pleasure in realizing that while each design appears here for the first time it already, in another sense, has a history. For those who are challenged to make their own decisions or create their own histories based on these designs, the modular approach that Maggie Lane has developed for her other books is a feature of this volume as well and enables readers to make innumerable adaptations, selecting borders perhaps from one design and central fields from another and, of course, following their own preferences in the choice of colors.

The five panels and seven rugs that are offered in this volume are certainly among Maggie Lane's outstanding achievements, both in scale and complexity. At the same time, they give us all that we have come to expect from her work. As in her earlier designs, we find again her sensitive adaptation of familiar Chinese shapes and themes, the same subtle but unmistakable opulence in large central figures, whether animal or man, and that celebration of color that has become the signature of a Maggie Lane design. Who begins this book, in short, begins not simply a book of patterns but an apprenticeship in the *art* of needlepoint.

M. P. Shaughnessy
Dean, City University of New York

The Chinese almanac calls 1976 the Year of the Dragon. To commemorate the occasion I give you here a poem Mina Shaughnessy wrote after she first viewed the dragon rug I made many years ago.

But before you read on, let me say to those of you who wanted to work that particular design, which appeared on the jacket of *Needlepoint by Design*, I will never make a graph of it. I painted the creature directly on the canvas. And I am sorry to say that although I wanted to graph the rug, I found that pedaling in reverse, so to speak, from finished stitches to little squares on graph paper proved to be a task too monumental for me to perform. I know, because I tried and failed. If I had drawn on the rug horizontal and vertical lines every tenth row to key the rug to the graph paper I might have succeeded. I decided, however, not to take that course.

Instead I have graphed another beast with the hope that he will appease and please the many disappointed dragon fanciers who wrote to me asking for a graph of the first dragon rug and who received in reply my regrets that I could not fill their needs.

And so, in honor of this year, 4674 in the ancient Chinese calendar—a year which will be one of prosperity, peace, harmony, and noble deeds, if you believe Chinese almanacs—my substitute dragon appears on pages 80–81, and Mina's original poem appears opposite.

Morning Walk

I meet each morning on my way to town
A scalloped dragon with a curly frown.
He's not symbolic or mythological;
If anything, he looks a little comical:
A head quite small in proportion to the tail,
Which often thwacks against a garbage pail
As he sweeps his serpent rind along the walk
Or rolls it up to punctuate his talk.
A Bunsen flame burns mildly at his joints
But his tongue licks out in blaze-red points
To help cool off the bonfire of his heart.
And despite my hesitations at the start—
For many of the people living here
Find my walking with a dragon rather queer—
The starting of my days would be too bare
If my undulating comrade were not there.

Mina Shaughnessy

Introduction

Those of you who are familiar with or have used *Chinese Rugs Designed for Needlepoint* will immediately recognize this book as its sequel. To you, the old hands, I address this opening chapter. Novices too, however, could profit by reading it. The succeeding chapters contain most of the information necessary for making the rugs, hangings, and panels presented here, but the following paragraphs may also prove helpful.

Step-by-step instructions will seldom accompany any graph in this book. I am sure the experienced worker has already found it most practical to begin a large piece of needlework near its center, since empty canvas is easier to grip than canvas already filled with stitches. Among the designs I give you here, however, only three, all of them rugs, have a central medallion, the logical starting point. Therefore you can start any of the other canvases wherever fancy dictates as long as you don't start at the edge.

All the graphs in this collection can be followed using only the basketweave stitch. In most of the rugs this plain, serviceable stitch was used because it takes wear better than stitches with long surface threads. In the wall panels and hangings, on the other hand, many stitches were used in order to simulate various natural textures. Since the decorative pieces were not meant to be walked upon, it seemed appropriate to use the ornamental stitches for the interesting effects they create.

If you decide to follow the sample panels or hangings and use the textured stitches, you can simplify your work if you first outline each area to be covered with such a stitch. With a thin thread of the color to be used in the ornamental stitch, run a single row of continental stitch around the area you will fill later. Work this row of stitches immediately *within* the outline given on the graph. You will then work the filling stitch over this almost invisible guide line and in so doing make it disappear completely.

Before beginning work on any canvas on which you want to leave the selvage, clip this edge every 2″. You need cut only through the tightly woven part, so use just the points of your scissors for each ½″ snip. This will permit the canvas's edge to stretch along with its surface, which always gives as you work on it. Then when you have completed your rug or panel, blocking it will be a relatively simple process, since the canvas will have a flat, evenly stitched surface. The section on blocking (page 7) gives complete instructions on this part of finishing a piece of needlepoint.

Most of the designs in this book have been worked with few colors and tones. Even so, you can make your hours of needlework more relaxing and enjoyable if you color the graph you are going to follow before you begin to work its design on the canvas. You need only shade in the faintest echoes of the colors you plan to use in your work. With frets you may find it almost impossible to read the graph without the help of a second tone. Use colored pencils for tinting the graphs. When kept sharp and used with a light touch they can produce a most attractive breath of color on the page.

Paternayan's three-ply Persian wool was used for most of the panels and hangings and for all the rugs in this book. Since you will want to keep your skeins of cut yarn neat, loop them once so that all the cut ends lie together. Tie each bundle twice, once near the looped end and once near the cut ends. Whenever you want a new thread, pull from the looped end of the hank.

A. D. Marker pens are excellent for drawing graph lines on needlepoint canvas. Dark tan is the color I use for both ecru and white canvas.

2

Eternal Knot Rug   see pages 18-23

Camel and Rider Hanging   see pages 24-33

Lichee Nut Panel   see pages 34-41

Geometric Rug
see pages 42-59

Sacred Mountain Rug
see pages 60-67

Double Dragon Medallion Rug   see pages 68-77

Dragon and Butterflies Panel   see pages 78-91

Mongolian Archer Hanging
see pages 92-105

Money II Rug   see pages 106-111

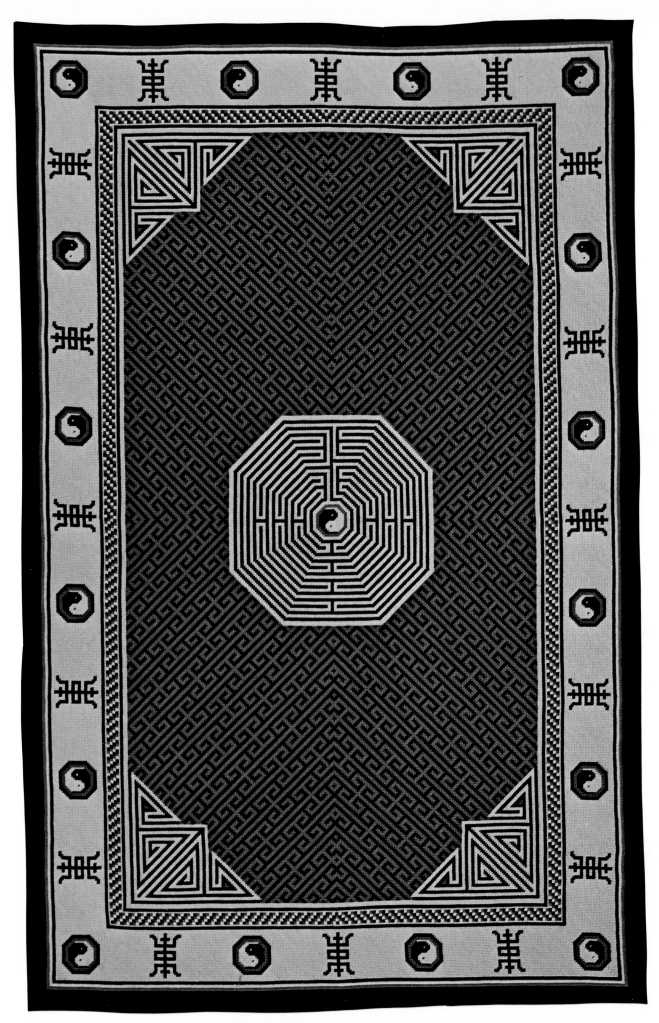

Maze and Fretwork Rug see pages 118-123

Deer and Crane Rug
see pages 112-117

Regal Eagle Hanging Scroll
see pages 124-133

To the Novice

For those of you who have never made a piece of needlepoint with only a graph as your guide, let me here explain the process.

The graphs in this book represent designs where every stitch has been finished and occupies its proper place. If you look closely at a piece of needlepoint you will observe a gridwork of fine, slightly wavy horizontal and vertical lines running up, down, and across its surface. This grid outlines the stitches. Each stitch looks like an oval grain of rice perched, slightly tilted, in the grid. A graph is simply a mechanical version of a piece of finished work. Instead of the slightly wavy gridlines visible on a piece of needlepoint, a graph presents straight, ironed-out gridlines that outline small squares rather than oval stitches. Many people are confused by a graph, thinking that the gridlines represent canvas threads. *They do not.* I repeat: the graph represents a finished piece of needlepoint where the canvas threads have all been covered and are no longer visible. Only the stitches can be seen. *The small squares on the graph represent stitches.* When you work needlepoint from a graph you are doing needlepoint by the numbers. Each square on the graph is meant to be worked as a stitch on your canvas.

After reading and comprehending the above paragraph you will immediately see that marking your canvas with lines corresponding to the heavy lines on the graph would simplify the counting process. The heavy graph lines occur every tenth line. Draw corresponding lines on your canvas. *Draw them between the canvas threads.* Allow 10 canvas threads between lines. When you have completed marking your canvas you will find that one large outlined square on your canvas will contain room for 100 stitches, just as each large block on the graph contains 100 small squares, each representing a finished stitch.

To help keep you from getting lost when reading from graph to canvas, you can key one to the other by numbering and lettering the rows of large blocks on both graph and canvas. Along both sides of the graph and both sides of the work area on the canvas, number the horizontal rows of blocks, and, at the top and bottom of the graph and the top and bottom of the work area on the canvas, letter the vertical rows of blocks.

The graph thread count is given at the beginning of the second paragraph of each set of instructions accompanying a graph. When the thread count is uneven—that is, when the numbers are odd numbers—mark the centers of your canvas *along* the horizontal and vertical center threads of your canvas. When the thread count is even—that is, when the numbers are even numbers—mark the centers of your canvas *between* two threads at the horizontal and vertical centers of your canvas. Bind your canvas with masking tape, or make a narrow folded hem on each side of your canvas, and sew it flat, either by machine or by hand. Otherwise the yarn or thread you use for work will constantly snag on the rough edges of your canvas. The canvas will also unravel if you do not bind it.

Use a needle with an eye big enough for easy threading. The size will vary according to the mesh of the canvas on which you plan to work. I find #16 to be a comfortable needle size for both #8 and #10 mesh canvas, but I suggest that you experiment and find the needle size that suits your needs best.

Some of you may find the graphs in the book a little too small for easy reading. If this is the case, a photostat of any graph can be enlarged to provide you with a larger grid and easier reading.

When you are ready to make the first stitch on your canvas, I strongly recommend that you mark, on the graph, the block of stitches containing your starting point. Then locate the corresponding block of stitches on your canvas. *Mark it immediately.* (Park a needle in it.) Otherwise you may, while threading your work needle, lose the place and have to find it all over again. If, in spite of checking and double-checking the location of the starting point, you find that you are off by a whole block, do not despair. There is a remedy. (And it is not ripping!) You can simply redraw the center lines and the outlines of your work area to allow for your error. This is one good reason for leaving several inches of blank canvas around the outlines originally drawn.

Canvas

Needlepoint canvas comes in several widths. Those of interest to the rug maker are 36″ wide, 40″ wide, and 60″ wide. To my knowledge, no one makes a canvas wider than 60″. If you want to make a rug much wider than 54″ (allowing 3″ extra on either side, which brings the total width to 60″) you will need to piece it. *None of the designs as graphed in this book require piecing.* Each one has been designed to be worked on an existing canvas width.

If you plan to graph or make your own rug designs, or to rescale one of the designs in this book, using a different canvas mesh than that used in the sample rug, the following set of figures will help you. It gives the *usable* thread-count for existing canvases along with each canvas's mesh size and width:

510 Usable threads	— #10 mono canvas	60″ wide
490 ,, ,,	— #9 Penelope canvas*	60″ ,,
465 ,, ,,	— #8 Penelope canvas*	60″ ,,
300 ,, ,,	— #10 mono canvas	36″ ,,
270 ,, ,,	— #9 Penelope canvas*	36″ ,,
270 ,, ,,	— #5 Penelope Quick-point	60″ ,,
240 ,, ,,	— #8 Penelope canvas*	36″ ,,
210 ,, ,,	— #7 Penelope canvas	36″ ,,

* If not available, use #10.

Tips on Working

When working on a rug use only those stitches that least distort a canvas. I recommend the basketweave and the brick stitch. *Never use the continental stitch* except for single rows of stitching where no other stitch can be used. The continental stitch distorts canvas so much that it is *totally* inappropriate for a piece of needlework that will be expected to remain rectangular without the help of a frame or some other form of rigid support.

Use as many strands of wool as you need to cover the canvas with an easy stitch—that is, a stitch made without a tug to tighten it. If you work with a hard pull at the end of each stitch, no amount of blocking can permanently correct the final result —a crooked canvas. Such a piece of work will stay rectangular *only* if mounted on a rigid frame that counteracts the tension you have created with your repeated tugging. A rug is destined to lie freely on the floor. Be kind to it when you work on it. Work with an easy, flowing rhythm and a stitch that does little to distort a rectangle. Again I repeat, *do not tug hard at your wool after every stitch*. If you follow these suggestions, your rug will need little blocking.

Do not allow your thread to twist and loop while you work. To keep it straight, roll the needle a bit after every stitch. You will soon discover how to do this. An untwisted thread makes for smoother stitches.

When you finish a thread, turn to the back of your work and run the needle and thread under almost a full needle's length of stitches before clipping off the thread's tail. Do the same when anchoring a new thread.

6

Finishing a Rug

(These instructions also apply to hangings and panels.)

During the entire period when I am working on a rug I press it almost daily, using a damp cloth and a hot iron. While doing this I pull the needlework to straighten it as much as possible. As a result, when the stitching on the rug has been completed, the finished piece is almost rectangular. But no matter how rectangular it appears, a rug should be blocked before being hemmed, bound, and lined.

Some needlepoint shops will perform these finishing services for you. However, if you want to finish a rug yourself, the following directions may be of help.

Blocking a Rug

Before blocking a rug, clip the selvages on the canvas unless you have already done so. (See page 2.) Lay the rug face down on a large wooden surface; a big table that you do not mind piercing with tacks or staples—or an area on a bare floor—or my solution, three boards, each ¾″ thick and measuring 30″ x 60″. When placed side by side on the floor they provide an ideal surface for blocking needlepoint. The total surface area measures 60″ x 90″. This size will accept the rugs or panels made on 60″ canvas. The lengthwise edges of the canvas will come to the edges of the wooden surface measuring 60″ x 90″. If you need a longer surface, add another 30″ x 60″ board to your collection. The boards can be stored upright in a closet where they will take up little space. If you wish to pad each board with muslin you will improve the surface on which you will be blocking your work.

Do not wet the rug before blocking it. This would only cause it to tighten up and go askew, making the blocking process very difficult, if not impossible. Instead, tack the dry canvas to the boards. The 3″ border of raw canvas that you left around your work will now perform part of its function.

Tack or staple one end and one side of the canvas to your boards. I use a #101 Swingline staple gun and staples with legs 5/16″ long. Put the staples in close to the edge of the canvas. Then they will not get wet and rust. Do not pull the canvas too hard as you stretch it—just enough to get out the ripples. Then anchor the free corner of the canvas, pulling fairly hard before you finally shoot in a few staples. These will probably have to come out later, for you will find that blocking a rug is a process of constant correction. A screwdriver is helpful for lifting up staples that need to be removed, but I have found that a pair of small stork-billed pliers removes the staples better than any other kind of tool.

Staple the second long side of the canvas, pulling as you go to keep it parallel with the edge of the wooden surface and the lengthwise edge of the canvas already stapled down. Finally staple the loose end of the canvas to the boards. This part of the process is the most difficult because you must see to it that all four corners of the needlepoint are square, that both sides measure the same number of inches in length, and that both ends also measure the same number of inches in width. If you see any waviness in the edges of your needlepoint, pull the canvas to eliminate the scalloped effect. I find that when I have finished stapling the canvas to the boards, the staples are quite close to each other; not much more than an inch separates one from the next.

At this point dampen the rug thoroughly. I spray mine, using water in a plastic bottle equipped with a squeezable handle and an adjustable nozzle that allows me to force out a fine, even mist. When the rug looks as though a heavy dew has fallen on it, take a damp cloth and an iron set at "Wool" and gently press the needlework. You can repeat the spraying and pressing as often as you like, but do not remove the rug from the boards until it is bone dry, at least 24 hours after the last steaming. If the rug remains rectangular after removal from its rigid supports, it is ready for hemming, binding, and lining.

Sizing a Rug (Optional)

Rex wallpaper paste can be used to size the back of any rug or hanging that needs help to remain rectangular. Mix the powdered paste with water, following the instructions given on the package. Brush the paste on the back of the rug, using a stiff paintbrush. Allow the sized rug to dry for at least 4 days. If some of the paste seeps through the canvas and wool and is visible when the rug is dry, scrub the rug's surface with a dry nail brush, then vacuum the resulting dust.

The effects of too much sizing will be more visible on the surface of a predominantly dark rug than on one with a medium to pale background.

Sizing will help your rug to remain neat and rectangular for a period of time, but if and when the paste cracks and turns into dust, the rug may eventually need reblocking or resizing.

Hemming a Rug

Trim unwanted excess canvas from the edges of your finished needlework. Leave 2″ for hemming. Lay the rug face down and turn each corner of the unworked canvas in toward the rug. Stop turning when you see the corner of the worked area. Press this flap. Cut off the excess part of the turned-in canvas flap, cutting parallel to the diagonal fold line. Leave an inch between cutting line and fold line. Then turn the four 2″ raw canvas hem allowances toward the back of the rug. Press. Where the four hem allowances meet diagonally at the corners, you have what is known as a mitered corner. Sew these diagonal corner seams, using button and carpet thread. Talon makes it in color 506, which is exactly the color of ecru canvas. Use the

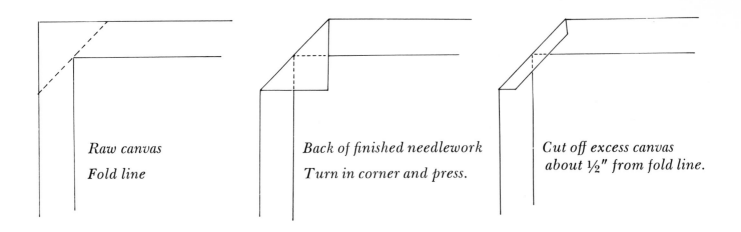

Raw canvas

Fold line

Back of finished needlework

Turn in corner and press.

Cut off excess canvas about ½" from fold line.

same kind of thread and a back stitch to sew the four hems to the under side of your rug. (Do not pick up more than wool on the back of your rug when you sew the hems to it. You do not want the thread to show on the surface of your work.)

Turn the rug over. There should be no raw canvas showing. The edges should be straight and flat and the corners neat and true.

Binding a Rug

Take a skein of wool. *Cut it once.* Thread your needle; pull the thread halfway through so that the thread hangs from the needle's eye in two tails of equal length. Turn the point of the needle back on the tails and pierce both of them as close to the needle as possible. Draw the needle through the pierced threads. Smooth the joining of the threads. You now have a double thread that will not slip in the needle's eye. This method of threading a needle with a double tail is better than putting two threads through the needle's eye, because with this method you have less bulk to pull through the canvas, having only one thread rather than two in the needle's eye.

Begin the binding of your rug at a corner. Run the needle in and out a few times on the canvas hem under the rug. Back stitch once or twice if you want to anchor the thread more firmly. Bring the needle up at the corner and begin binding. Hold the rug with its edge up and the under side of your needle-

10

At edge of needlework, turn in one side of canvas and press.

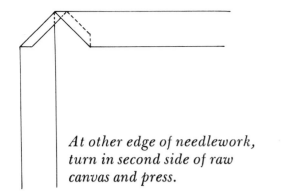

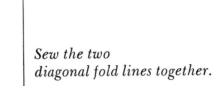

Sew the two diagonal fold lines together.

At other edge of needlework, turn in second side of raw canvas and press.

work toward you. Make stitches from the right side of the rug toward the under side. The binding will whip and wrap the first row of needlepoint and the first row of raw canvas underneath. Work over each edge stitch on top and through each matching hole underneath, making a snug, even spiral. The double whipping thread will produce a neat, rolled edge. Keep the whipping threads from twisting and do not pull them too hard as you work or you will produce a rippled edge. When casting off the ends of the whipping threads, or anchoring new ones, weave the ends into the raw canvas as described earlier. Continue whipping, casting off, and beginning new threads until you have whipped a rolled edge around the entire rug.

Lining a Rug

Buy a piece of heavy cotton, like duck or sailcloth, or a piece of tightly woven linen, preferably of a neutral beige color. Cut this to a size about 4″ longer and 4″ wider than your bound rug. Fold in 2″ along two adjoining sides of the lining. Miter the resulting corner, cutting off the excess triangle of fabric to eliminate bulk. Lay the rug face down on a flat surface. Place the lining on the back of the rug so that the two turned edges of the lining meet the binding on two edges of your rug. Pin the lining to the bound edges. Then turn under the remaining two sides of the lining so they meet the other two whipped edges of the rug. Miter the unmitered corners of the lining. Pin the lin-

11

ing to the bound rug along the two free sides. Then catch stitch the lining to the binding all the way around the rug.

While the rug is still lying face down, tack the lining to the rug by means of a row of basting stitches running all the way around the sides of the rectangle, but 2″ from the bound edges. Then tack the center of the lining to the center of the rug, using a large horizontal and vertical cross stitch and a large diagonal cross stitch. These tacking stitches will keep the lining from creeping and showing around the edges of the rug, once it lies face up on the floor.

NOTE   It is wise to place a piece of rubber matting under your needlepoint rug to keep it from slipping on the floor. (Small rugs that slip when walked on can cause terrible accidents.) The matting should be about 4″ narrower and 4″ shorter than the rug. To keep the rug and the matting properly aligned, tack the ends of four strips of tape laid diagonally across the under-side corners of your rug. Slip the corners of the matting into these traps. Or make four triangular pockets for the four under-side corners of your rug. Sew them to the rug lining about an inch in from the corner edges of the rug. Slip the corners of the matting into these pockets.

Finishing a Hanging

I have used the word "hanging" wherever there is no rigid support for the canvas, i.e., where the canvas hangs free. I have used "panel" wherever the canvas has been mounted on an invisible wooden support or stretcher.

You need not bind or line hangings or panels. It is advisable, however, to block and steam the hangings. Turn back the hems and miter the corners before catching the hems to the back of the needlework.

A carpenter can make the wooden frame for a panel. He should make it with a narrow raised rim along the four outer edges on the front side of the stretcher so that the stitched part of the mounted canvas touches wood only where it crosses this rim. If the panel is quite large, ask the carpenter to put one or two supports or struts like railway ties between the long sides of the stretcher. This will help keep the stretcher from warping or going askew.

Before you take the measurements of a piece of finished needlework, stretch the canvas on a wooden surface, being sure to eliminate all ripples in the work. *If the piece has been stitched in silk do not wet it.* (If it has been worked in wool, steam and press it if you feel that doing so will improve the appearance of the work.) Only after stretching the canvas should measurements be taken. These are the exact dimensions you should give to the carpenter.

Mounting a panel provides no problem for a person familiar with stretching primed canvas on which to paint a picture. For those who have never tackled such a task, however, let me suggest that you begin by marking the center of each of the four sides of the wooden stretcher. Place the four center lines already marked on your canvas against the marks on the frame. Turn the raw canvas around your work back along the sides of the stretcher. Staple this raw canvas to the frame's sides. Start from the four center points and work toward the four corners. Work all four sides concurrently—that is, drive a few staples to the left of the center staple at the top of the panel. Drive in a few staples to the right of the same center staple. Repeat this process on the bottom of your panel. Follow the same process on both sides of the panel. From this point on, keep working from the centers toward the corners, always driving in only a few staples at a time so that you keep the tension of the needlepoint even. When you reach the four corners, fold the excess canvas so that it presents as little bulk as possible.

Once this part of the mounting process has been completed, fold toward the back of the frame the excess canvas still remaining around the panel, and staple it flat to the stretcher, doing so all the way around the back of the panel.

You can now remove the staples on all four sides of the panel, those used in the first step of mounting. The panel should show, at this point, smooth, taut needlepoint across its surface and raw canvas along its four sides. The staples on the back are, of course, invisible when the panel is hung. If you do not like the look of raw canvas on the top, bottom, and sides of the panel, you can cover it with twill tape or any kind of concealing material you think appropriate. Ecru canvas around the four sides of a panel pleases me, however, so I never try to hide it.

Buying Wool

A skein of 3-ply Persian wool weighs about a quarter of a pound and will cover approximately one square foot of canvas. When ordering wool for a rug the only quantity you need worry about is that of the color you will be using in the background. Nevertheless, before you begin to work on your rug, try to buy at one time all the wool you will need for the project. If you run short of any of the colors used in patterned or figured areas, do not worry. Simply buy more as the need arises. *Different dye lots will not be apparent when used in these areas.* But in the background even the slightest difference in tone or color that can occur in wools dyed in different lots can cause a problem. Even so a remedy of sorts is available to you. If you find your supply of background color is not going to be enough to finish the area that must be covered, save some of the wool you are using, order more, and when the new wool arrives, take one strand of the new and add it to the old, removing one strand of the old. Work with this combination of new and old for a few rows. Then use two strands of new in place of two strands of old. Work for another few rows. Finally, use all new wool. This process will help soften a change of tone or color that might be quite apparent if you made an abrupt change from one dye lot to another.

The Patterns

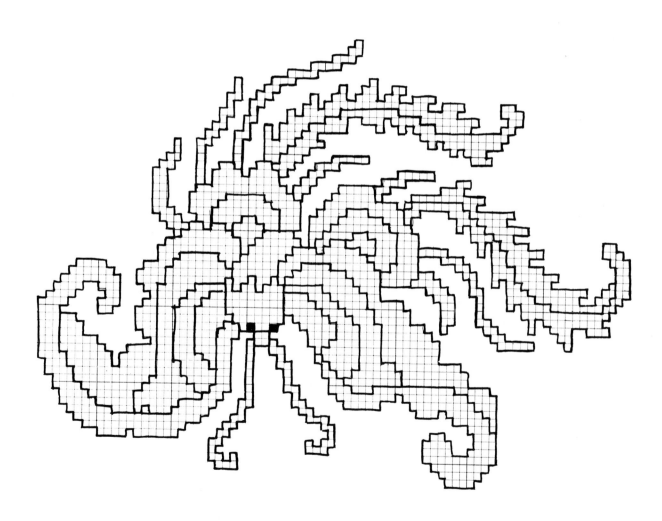

Eternal Knot Rug

27" x 51"

Worked on #12 mono canvas

This design was adapted from a Kansu saddle rug, plate 70 in *A View of Chinese Rugs* by H. A. Lorentz (Routledge and Kegan Paul Ltd., publishers, London).

The graph thread count is 301 x 607. Bind a piece of #12 mono canvas measuring 34" x 58". Mark the horizontal and vertical center threads and outline the entire work area. Mark graph lines.

The sample rug was made with Persian wool, using two strands for the basketweave (page 136) in the eternal knots and dotted border band, and using three strands for the Irish stitch (page 137) in the background of the field and border.

Three tones and colors were used in the Eternal Knot rug. The key follows:

017 Off-white	2 lbs.
381 Medium blue	¼ lb.
365 Navy blue	1 lb.

Outline the eternal knots in the field, using 381 medium blue. Fill in the eternal knots with 365 navy blue. Then work a single row of white continental stitch around each knot.

Work the dotted border around the field. Work the single row of white near the outer edge of the rug. Work the white eternal knots in the border. Outline each knot with a single row of navy-blue continental stitch.

Fill in the field with the Irish stitch. Work it so that the stitch threads lie parallel to the short sides of the canvas. A single row of white continental stitch at each end of the field will keep the Irish stitch from rolling into and partially obscuring the first row of the dotted border.

Fill in the border with the Irish stitch. Work the long sides of the rug border with the stitches going in the same direction as the stitches in the field. Work the short sides of the rug border with the stitch direction at a right angle to the stitch direction in the field. The stitches meet at the four corners of the rug and give the appearance of a mitered corner. A diagonal line drawn at each corner of the rug, from the rug's outer corner to the field's outer corner, will help you when you work the Irish-stitch border background, showing you where to change the direction of your stitch.

This rug would be equally attractive worked with off-white eternal knots on a navy-blue field and navy-blue eternal knots in an off-white border.

The sample rug was worked by June Shankland Hilliker.

Camel and Rider Hanging

30″ x 62″

Worked on #12 mono canvas

This hanging was adapted from a Chinese stringed instrument called a p'i-p'a. The T'ang dynasty antique that provided the inspiration for my design was shaped like a lute. It was made of wood, then lacquered across its waist where the camel and rider were then inlaid in mother-of-pearl.

The graph thread count is 319 x 722. The upper and lower parts of the hanging are 319 x 161. The central part is 319 x 400. Bind a piece of #12 mono canvas measuring 36″ x 68″. Mark the center lines and outline the entire work area. Mark the lines dividing the three sections of the hanging. On the upper and lower parts of the hanging, outline the rectangles for the repeat motif. In each of these rectangles mark the horizontal and vertical center threads. Mark the graph lines only in the central part of the hanging.

The sample hanging was made with Persian wool. Work the taupe areas on the camel in the French double-tied stitch (page 139) using one strand of wool.

Work the rest of the camel in horizontal rows of Smyrna cross stitch (page 139) using two strands of wool.

Work the end of the camel's tail in the double Leviathan stitch (page 137) using two strands of wool.

Work the three ornaments on the camel's harness in the ribbed wheel (page 138) using two strands of wool.

Work the rider, the saddle, the musical instrument, and the flowers in the upper and lower parts of the hanging in basketweave, using two strands of wool.

Work the background of the center part of the hanging in the Irish stitch (page 137) using three strands of wool.

Work the background of the upper and lower parts of the hanging in the patterned flat stitch (page 140) using three strands of wool.

Four tones and colors were used in the Camel and Rider hanging. The key follows:

010 White	1 lb.
Taupe (special dye)	1 lb.
105 Tête de Nègre	1 lb.
527 Green	¼ lb.

The sample hanging was worked by Maggie Lane.

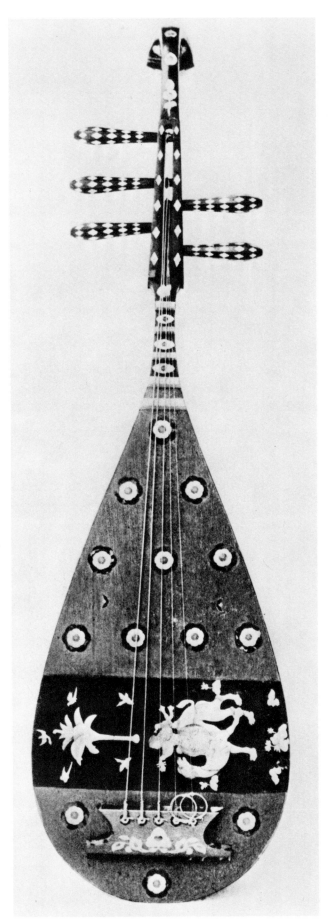

A Chinese p'i p'a. Reproduced from
The Chinese Collector Through the Centuries
by Michel Beurdeley.
Charles E. Tuttle Co., Inc., 1966.

Design continues on next spread.

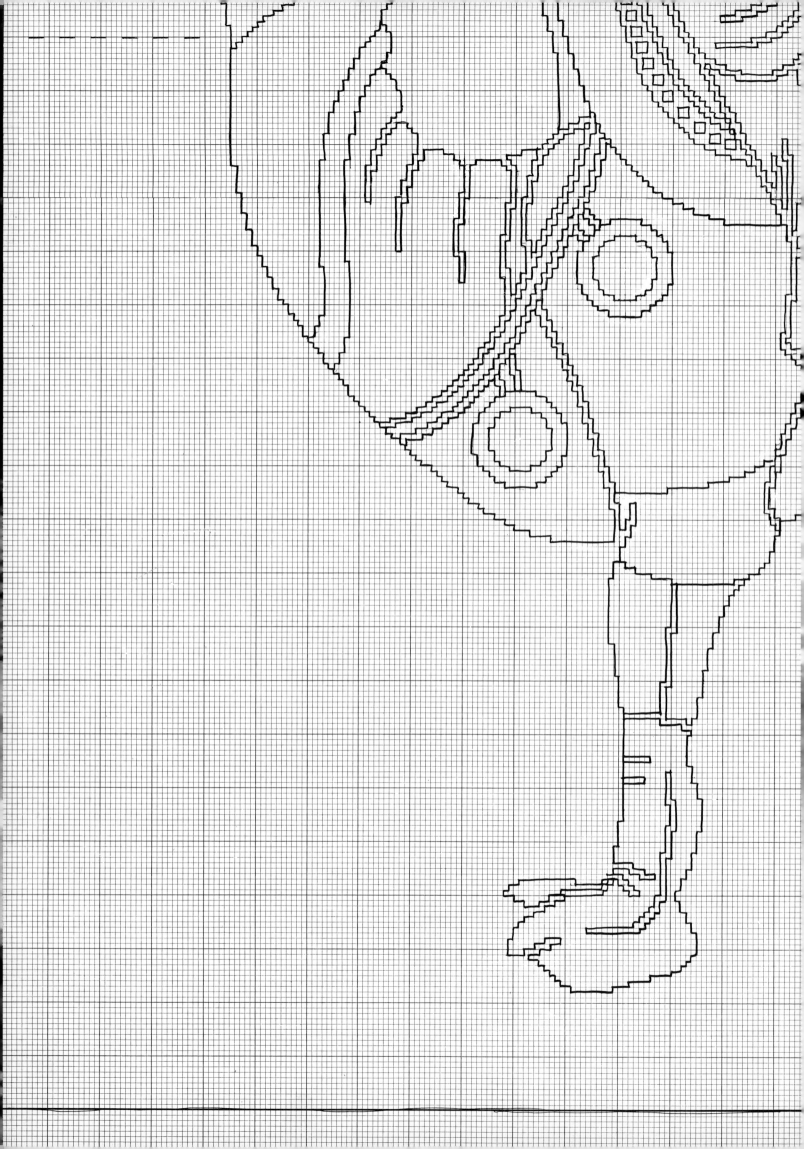

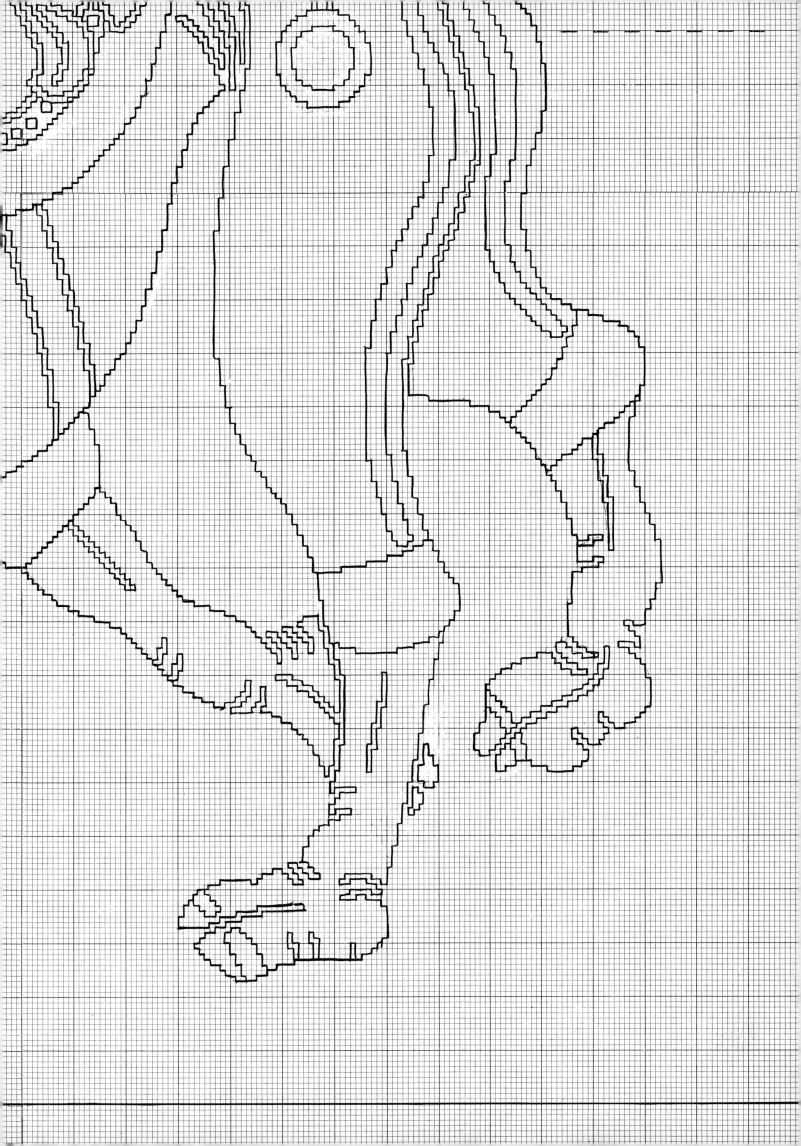

Lichee Nut Panel

31" x 32"

Worked on #12 mono canvas

This design was adapted from a fifteenth-century Chinese carved lacquer tray.

The graph thread count is 381 x 381. (The finished panel measures 31" x 32" because canvas is not woven so that the distance between horizontal threads is exactly the same as the distance between vertical threads. Multiply the slight difference by 381 and the result is a rectangle an inch longer than it is wide.) Bind a piece of #12 canvas measuring 36" x 36". Mark the horizontal and vertical center threads and outline the entire work area. Mark the graph lines in the tray area.

NOTE For this panel I would suggest using a drawing pencil rather than a pen for marking the graph lines. The reason is that many of the stitches in the lichee nuts are pulled thread stitches. Any dark graph lines will show through the pulled threads. Lines made with colored pencil rather than pen can be removed with cleaning fluid and a Q-tip. This should be done after the lichee nut has been outlined with a single row of continental stitch worked with a very thin thread, two or three strands of silk, and before you work the lichee nut in an ornamental stitch. The best color of pencil to use is one as close as possible to the color of your canvas.

The sample panel was made with Medici wool, using five strands, and Au Ver à Soie silk, using the seven strands that cling together to form one thread. (For some stitches filling the lichee nuts, however, you will be using fewer strands.)

35

Six tones and colors were used in the Lichee Nut panel. The key follows:

309 Olive-brown wool (Medici)	5 skeins
200 Navy wool (Medici)	1 skein
3712 Pale celadon silk (Au Ver à Soie silk)	5 skeins
3713 Celadon silk (Au Ver à Soie silk)	5 skeins
3714 Dark celadon silk (Au Ver à Soie silk)	1 skein
614 Lacquer-red silk (Sacrificial red) (Au Ver à Soie silk)	4 skeins

The branches and leaves of the Lichee Nut panel and the frame of the tray are worked with olive-brown wool, and wherever the under side of a leaf is visible navy wool is used. The veins in the leaves are worked with the dark celadon silk. Each lichee nut shows a dark area where the stem joins the fruit. Work these areas with the dark celadon. Outline each lichee nut with a single row of continental stitch worked with two or three strands of the pale celadon silk. Work each lichee nut in a different stitch (pages 139–155). The number of strands used for each stitch is given in the text accompanying the diagram for that particular stitch as worked in the sample panel.

The tone-on-tone patterned area framing the tray is worked with the light celadon and the celadon silk. Use any pattern you like. I used one that I found on a tenth-century B.C. Chinese bronze caldron. The pattern is called a thunder design. (See page 58.)

The sample panel was worked by Maggie Lane.

NOTE   While I was working on the Lichee Nut panel I intended to hang it with lichee nut #1 on the left-hand side of the panel. Then one day I turned it 45 degrees to see how it would look with lichee nut #1 at the top of the panel. I liked it and decided to hang it that way. The stitches in the lichee nuts had already been worked, however; so when you compare the finished picture with the diagram, bear this confessional note in mind.

CENTER

CENTER

CENTER →

CENTER

Geometric Rug

34" x 67"

Worked on #10 mono canvas

This rug was adapted from several antique Chinese rugs. The patterns in the border were found in a variety of old carpets.

The graph thread count is 324 x 612. Bind a piece of #10 mono canvas measuring 40" x 70". Mark the horizontal and vertical center lines and outline the entire work area. In this design I do not believe it is necessary to mark the graph lines except in the coin lozenges. I suggest that you draw lines separating the various border bands, from the outer edges up to the outline of the field. Outline the lozenges. Then draw graph lines in each lozenge.

The sample rug was made with Persian wool, using the full thread, all three strands.

Seven tones and colors were used in the Geometric rug. The key follows:

010 Off-white	1 lb.
496 Cream	1/4 lb.
492 Wheat	1/4 lb.
382 Light blue	1/4 lb.
380 Blue	1/4 lb.
145 Cognac	1/4 lb.
110 Dark brown	1 1/2 lbs.

The rug is based on an even thread count, but the field is based on an odd thread count. Therefore, your field pattern will be off center by one thread, horizontally and vertically. Work the key fret first, since it is the only part of the rug border that must be symmetrical. Work the latticework in the field. Work the flowers. Then work the background around each flower.

Outline the lozenges. Work the coins and fluttering ribbons. Work the background of each lozenge.

Work the patterned areas between the lozenges. Use any of the patterns supplied for these areas, coloring them as you like.

Work the outer border.

The sample rug was worked in basketweave by Maggie Lane.

BOTTOM CENTER

Suggested designs for
patterned areas between
border lozenges

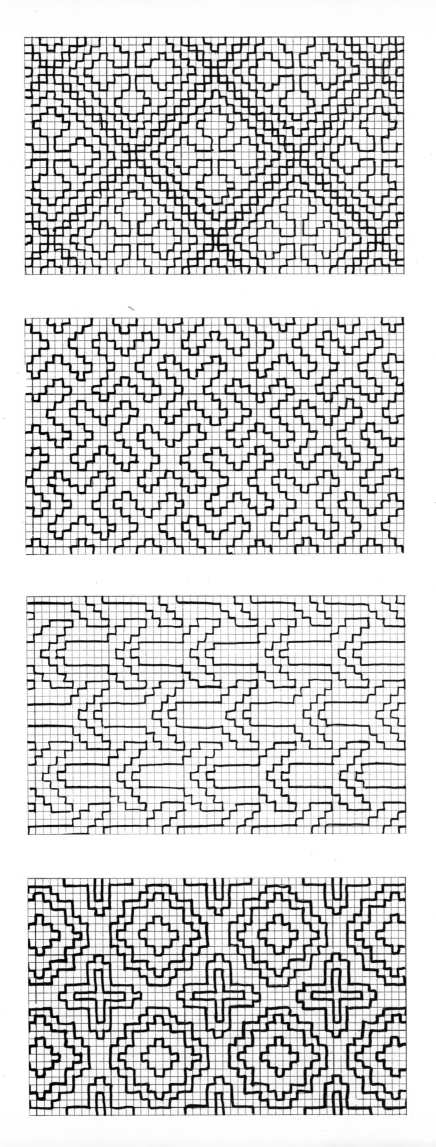

Suggested designs for patterned areas between border lozenges

Suggested designs for
patterned areas between
border lozenges

Suggested designs for
background patterns

Suggested designs for
background patterns

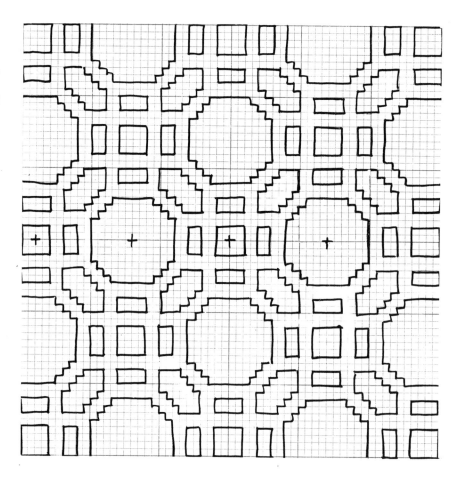

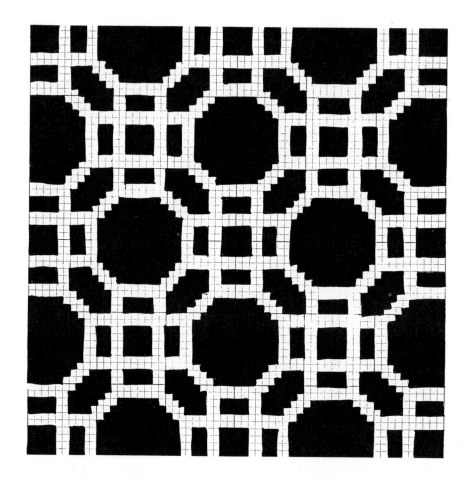

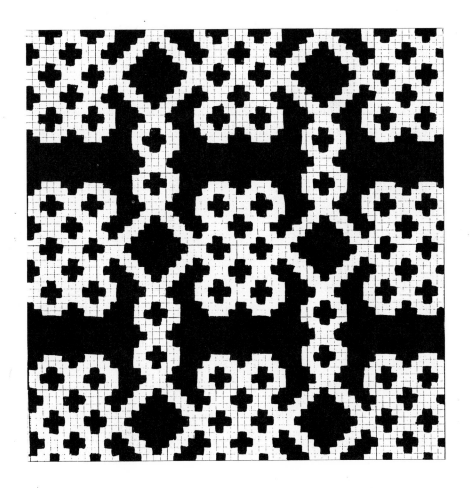

Suggested designs for
background patterns

Suggested designs for
background patterns

Sacred Mountain Rug

33" x 68"

Worked on #10 mono canvas

This design was adapted from an antique Chinese rug in the Victoria and Albert Museum, London.

The graph thread count is 317 x 641. Bind a piece of #10 mono canvas measuring 40" x 74". Mark the horizontal and vertical center threads and outline the entire work area. Mark the graph lines within the work area.

The sample rug was made with Persian wool using the full thread, all three strands.

Ten tones and colors were used in the Sacred Mountain rug. The key follows:

005 White	½ lb.
425 Light apricot	¾ lb.
430 Medium light apricot	½ lb.
420 Medium apricot	2 lbs.
225 Dark apricot	¼ lb.
90 Celadon gray (Nantucket Needleworks wool)	2 skeins
594 Light green	¼ lb.
560 Medium green	¼ lb.
124 Medium dark brown	½ lb.
114 Dark brown	1¼ lbs.

The sample rug was worked in basketweave by Barbara Brown Rubinstein.

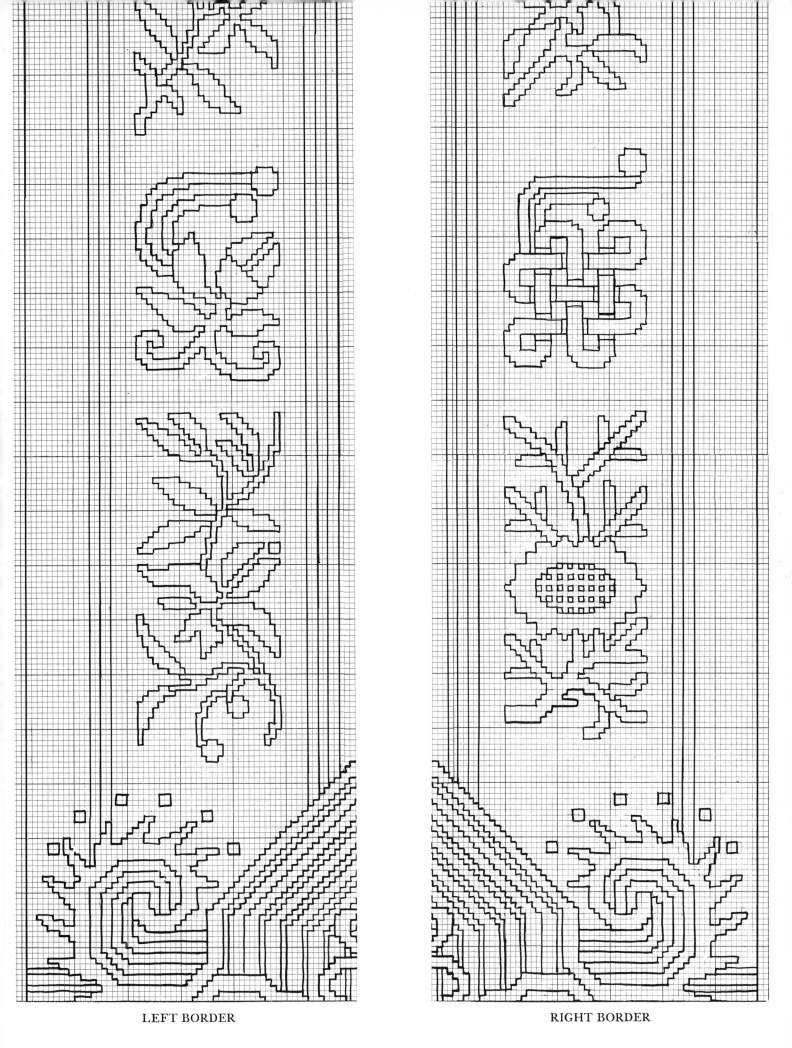

LEFT BORDER   RIGHT BORDER

Graphs to show borders of the Sacred Mountain Rug.
The borders are continued on pages 66 and 67.

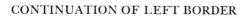

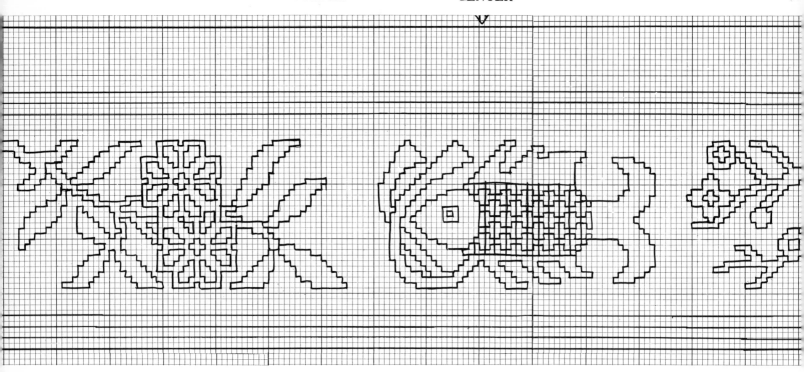

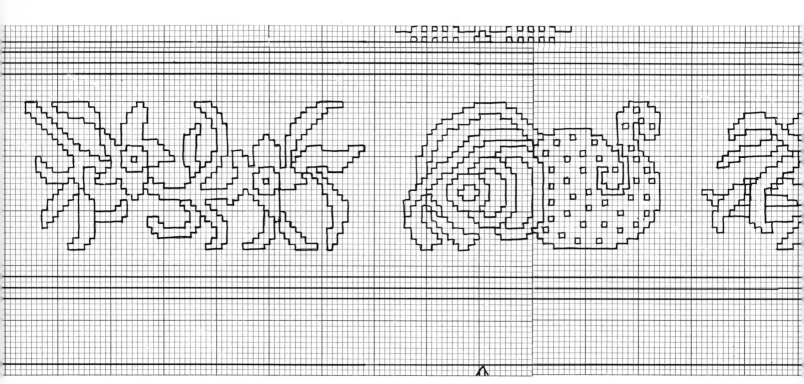

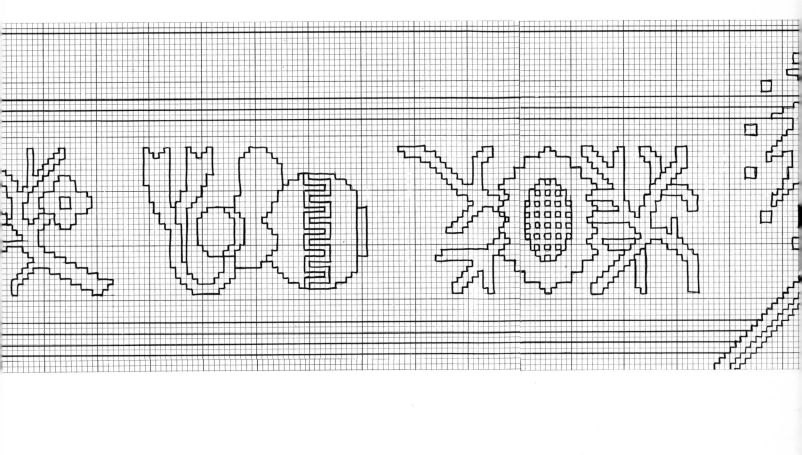

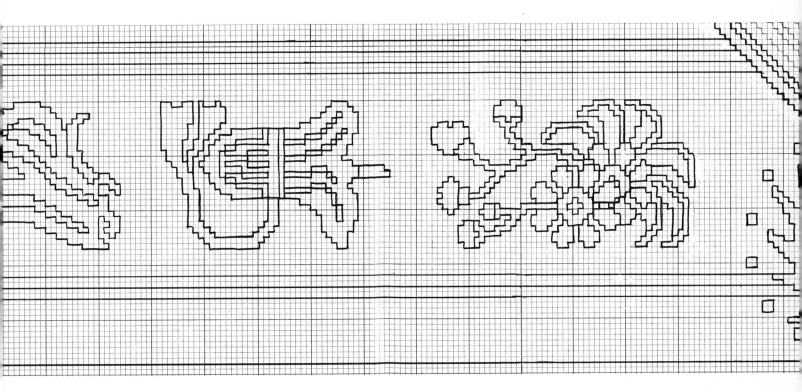

Double Dragon Medallion Rug
50" x 71"

Worked on #8 Penelope canvas

This design was adapted from an eighteenth-century Chinese carpet, plate 38 in *A View of Chinese Rugs* by H. A. Lorentz (Routledge and Kegan Paul Ltd., publishers, London). Archaic dragons and the eight Taoist symbols appear in the field.

The graph thread count is 402 x 570. Bind a piece of #8 Penelope canvas measuring 60" x 80". Mark the horizontal and vertical center lines, and outline the entire work area. Mark the graph lines in the field of the rug.

The sample rug was made with Persian wool, using the full thread, all three strands. If you want a rug with a tight weave, add one extra strand of wool to the three-strand thread. You will then be working with four strands.

Five tones and colors were used in the Double Dragon Medallion rug. The key follows:

012 Off-white	4½ lbs.
381 Pale blue	1 lb.
311 Medium blue	¾ lb.
492 Wheat	1 oz.
433 Amber	1 oz.

The sample rug was worked in basketweave (page 136) by Paul Griffith.

BOTTOM CENTER

Dragon and Butterflies Panel

54" x 80"

Worked on #8 Penelope canvas

The elements in this design were taken from several sources. I found the dragon on an embroidered hanging in the possession of my friend Florence Gustafson, who also owns the Chinese embroidered robe on which I found the butterflies. The upper and lower borders were taken from an antique Chinese jardinière. When designing the panel I wanted to create a kind of "spirit screen," an architectural device used by the Chinese to keep evil spirits and devils from entering their homes. In the old days, a Chinese residence was built in a compound surrounded by high stone walls. The pair of wooden doors in the gatehouse were usually locked. When they were opened, however, one walked through the front entrance only to be faced with an ornamental wall around either end of which one had to walk before actually being *in* the compound. Because the Chinese believed that spirits were unable to go around corners, such a wall or screen, like a baffle, kept the devils from entering a compound and tormenting the residents.

The graph thread count is 400 x 611. Bind a piece of #8 Penelope canvas measuring 60" x 86". Mark the vertical center line. Outline the entire work area. Mark the graph lines within the work area.

The panel was made with Persian wool, using three strands for all areas worked in basketweave.

There is no need to follow any particular sequence in working this panel. However, when working Smyrna cross-stitch areas in the dragon's hands and face, first outline these areas with a line of thin continental stitches, using a single strand of yarn in your needle. Cover these stitches when you work the rows of Smyrna cross stitches.

I would also suggest working the dragon's white spine and his white frontal crest, as well as those crusty lines around his front and hind legs, before working the scales on his body and legs. When working the scales, outline them in white, watching for their directional turns, which occur in the dragon's neck and chest and in his tail.

After outlining the scales, work the small diamond in the root of each scale. Use the second tone of green for this. Finally, fill in the scales with the lightest tone of green.

Shade the butterflies as you please.

The outline and background of the characters in the upper border were worked in the second tone of green. The thin lines in the waves at the bottom of the panel were worked with the palest tone of green.

The sample panel was worked by Maggie Lane.

Thirteen tones and colors were used in the Dragon and Butterflies panel. The key follows:

147	Light lavender	2 oz.
137	Medium light lavender	2 oz.
127	Medium lavender	2 oz.
117	Medium dark lavender	2 oz.
597	Light celadon green	1 lb.
594	Medium light celadon green	½ lb.
560	Medium celadon green	2 oz.
512	Medium dark celadon green	2 oz.
396	Light blue	2 oz.
395	Medium light blue	2 oz.
385	Medium dark blue	2 oz.
330	Dark blue	4 lbs.
010	White	1 lb.

The "hands" and face of the dragon, as well as the wide white band at the bottom of the panel, were worked in horizontal rows of Smyrna cross stitch (page 139) using two strands of wool.

LOWER LEFT CORNER

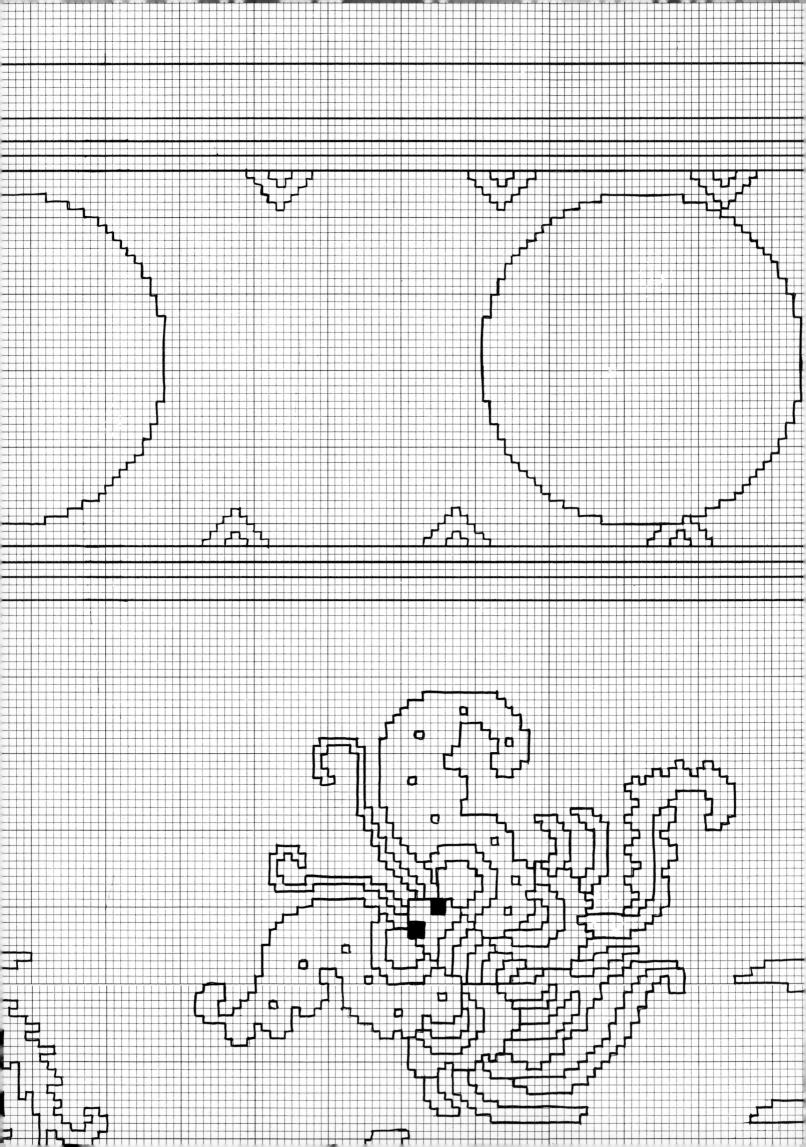

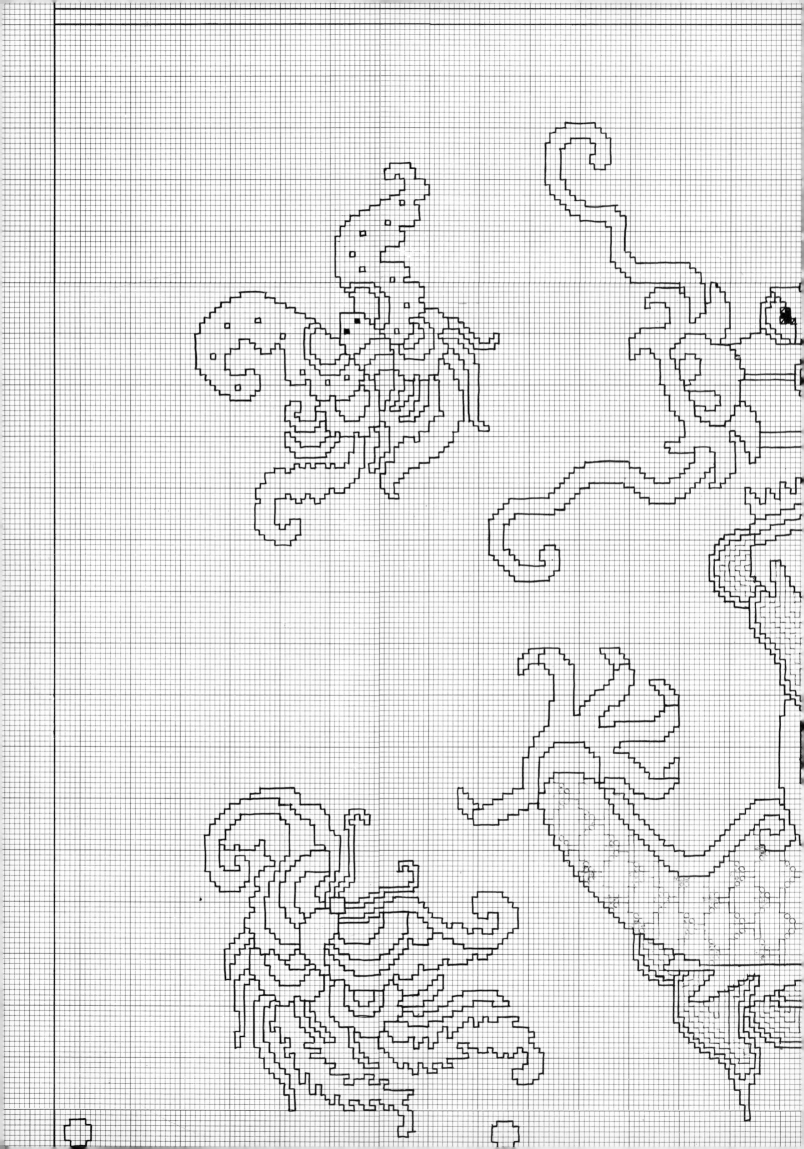

Pattern continued on following page

Space for Dragonfly, see page 90.

CENTER

CENTER

DRAGONFLY. For Dragon and Butterflies panel.

This part of the design is optional. It can be used only if the panel is worked on Penelope canvas where the grospoint double thread can be split for the dragonfly, which must be worked in petit point.

The dragonfly's position on the graph is indicated by four corner brackets drawn under the dragon's chest. The dragonfly must be worked in petit point using one strand of wool. Separate the double canvas threads, both horizontal and vertical, within the indicated area. Add the additional graph lines to accommodate the dragonfly graph. For the dragonfly's wings, use the double faggot stitch (page 155) using one strand of wool.

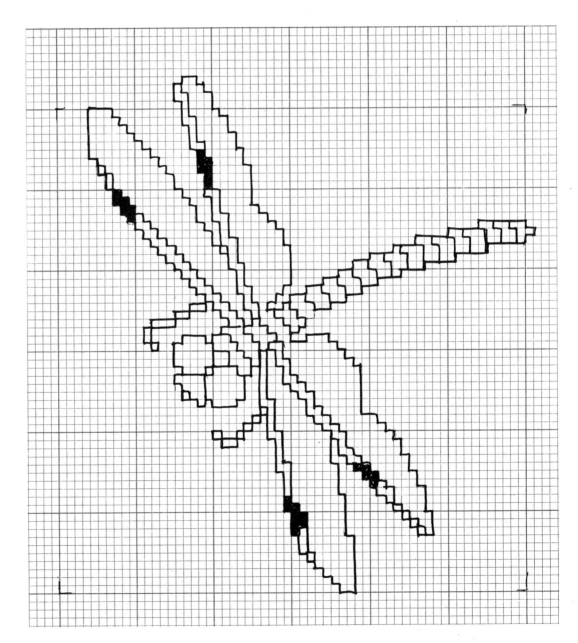

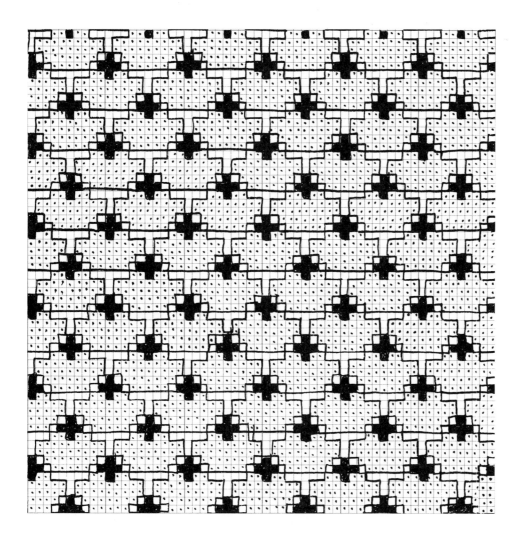

DRAGON SCALES

Mongolian Archer Hanging

29" x 72"

Worked on #12 mono canvas

This design was adapted from a Yüan dynasty painting by Chian Hsuan, A.D. 1290 (British Museum, London). A nineteenth-century Chinese pillar rug in the Royal Ontario Museum, Toronto, provided the details for the upper and lower parts of the hanging.

The graph thread count is 321 x 790. The length is divided into three parts. The count in the upper part is 321 x 135. The count in the central portion is 321 x 520. The count in the lower part is 321 x 135. Bind a piece of #12 mono canvas measuring 35" x 78". Outline the entire work area. Mark the lines dividing the work area into its three parts. Mark the graph lines in the central portion only.

Seventeen tones and colors were used in the Mongolian Archer hanging. The key follows:

012	White	¼ lb.
020	Beige-white	¼ lb.
573	Celadon	¼ lb.
583	Dark celadon	1 oz.
382	Light blue	1 oz.
380	Blue	¼ lb.
492	Straw	¼ lb.
136	Tan	1½ lbs.
248	Soft rosy brown	10 threads
225	Coral	¼ lb.
267	Dark coral	1 oz.

145 Tobacco brown	10 threads
286 Soft coral	20 threads
164 Gray	1 oz.
114 Dark brown	1½ lbs.
105 Tête de Nègre	2 oz.
050 Black	10 threads

The sample hanging was made with Persian wool.
Placement of stitches in the hanging:

Work the archer's tunic in Jacquard stitch (page 158) using two strands of wool.
Work the archer's boot in the Hungarian stitch (page 156) using two strands of wool. (Use celadon and dark celadon.)
Work the dots in the colored bands across the upper and lower parts of the hanging in Smyrna cross stitch (page 139) using two strands of wool.
Work the pony's saddle in the patterned flat stitch (page 157) using three strands of wool. (Use tête de Nègre for the lacework pattern of veins. Fill in the ovals with dark brown.)
Work the background of the central part of the hanging with the brick stitch (page 158) using three strands of wool.
Work the large areas of dark brown in the upper and lower parts of the hanging in the back-and-forth herringbone stitch (page 159) using three strands of wool.
All areas not listed above are worked in the basketweave stitch (page 136) using two strands of wool.

Placement of colors in the center part of the hanging:

1. For outlining flesh on the face, use 136 tan, the background color.
2. For flesh on face and neck use 020 beige-white. For lips and lines inside the ear, and for outlining flesh on arms and hands, use 286 soft coral.
3. For flesh on arms and hands use 020 beige-white.

4. For eyes, eyebrows, and hair use 050 black.
5. For hat use 105 tête de Nègre.
6. For outlining the tunic and for lines within it use 267 dark coral.
7. For tunic use 225 coral.
8. For boot use 573 and 583 celadon.
9. For bow string use 020 beige-white.
10. For belt and bow use 105 tête de Nègre.
11. For bridle on the pony use 380 blue.
12. For outlining the pony's eyes use 583 celadon.
13. For pupils of pony's eyes use 145 tobacco brown with 050 black pupils.
14. For the pony's nostrils use 248 soft rosy brown and 145 tobacco brown.
15. For the pony's mouth line use 248 soft rosy brown.
16. For outlines, and for lines within the four-leaf-clover pattern on the pony, use 012 white.
17. For filling in the clover pattern on the pony use 020 beige-white.
18. For drawing lines on the pony's body—i.e., at the chest, the stomach, and at the upper part of his front legs where one is seen against the other, and his back legs, again where one is seen against the other—use 164 gray.
19. For background of the pony's body use one strand of 573 celadon and one strand of 136 tan background color together in the needle if you want the slightly greenish tan I used. Otherwise, use two strands of 136 background color.
20. For the pony's hoofs use 164 gray.
21. For outlining the two cloud bands, one at the top and one at the bottom of the central part of the hanging, use 012 white.
22. For filling in the cloud bands use 492 straw.
23. For tassels use 012 white and 225 coral.
24. For the tassels on the pony's bridle use 225 coral and 267 dark coral.

Placement of colors in the upper and lower parts of the hanging:

1. For the multicolored band at the top edge of the upper part of the hanging and at the bottom edge of the lower part of the hanging, start with three rows of 136 tan. Then work the six-row band of 114 dark brown in the back-and-forth herringbone stitch.
2. Work two rows of 012 white.
3. Work two rows of 114 dark brown.
4. Work four rows of 136 tan with 012 white Smyrna cross stitch dots.
5. Work two rows of 382 light blue.
6. Work four rows of 380 blue with 012 white Smyrna cross stitch dots.
7. Work two rows of 136 tan. (This color keeps the blue and coral bands apart visually so that when seen from a distance your eye does not mix the coral with the blue, which would result in a purple tone.)
8. Work four rows of 225 coral with 012 white Smyrna cross stitch dots.
9. Work two rows of 114 dark brown.
10. Work two rows of 012 white.
11. Work the large area in 114 dark brown, using the back-and-forth herringbone stitch (page 159).

NOTE   For the two-row bands listed above I used two strands of wool and a diagonal satin stitch that covered the width of the band. I changed the direction of the diagonal slant from band to band in order to prevent distortion of the canvas. The white, coral, and brown bands next to the cloud bands at the top and bottom of the central part of the hanging are worked in 012 white, 225 coral, and 114 dark brown. Again, the white and coral bands are worked in a diagonal satin stitch, changing the direction of the slant from band to band to prevent distortion of the canvas.

The pattern penciled in on the pony's face is there as a clue to start you off with the clover-leaf pattern centered on his face. I did not draw the pattern in ink because it might become confusing in relation to the drawing of the eyes. For continued repeat of this pattern see page 50 (#4). You may want to work the pony without any pattern or you may prefer to use another one of the many repeat patterns accompanying the Geometric rug.

I have drawn in ink only a few lines to indicate how the curved striping on the tail should be worked; the balance of the tail striping has been drawn in pencil. The stripes in the pony's forelock have also been penciled within an inked outline, again to avoid confusion.

The sample hanging was worked by Maggie Lane and Paul Griffith.

To be used for upper and lower borders of the Mongolian Archer hanging. See page 92.

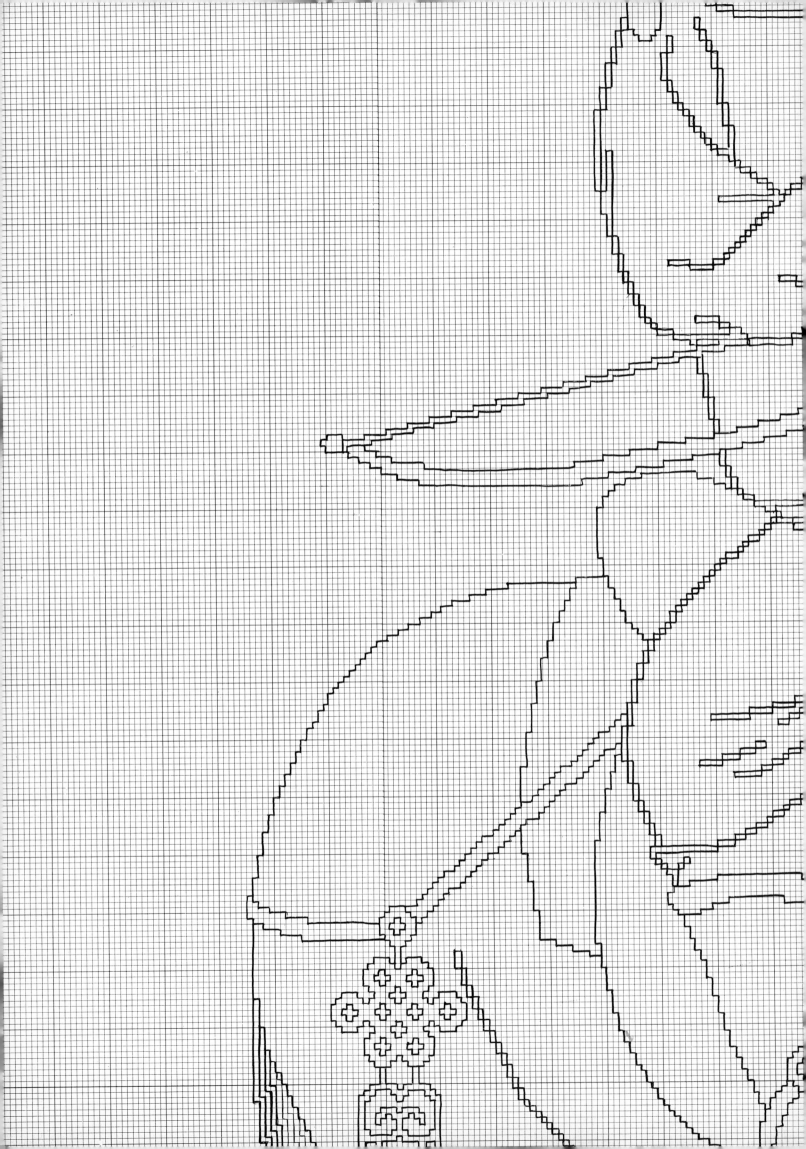

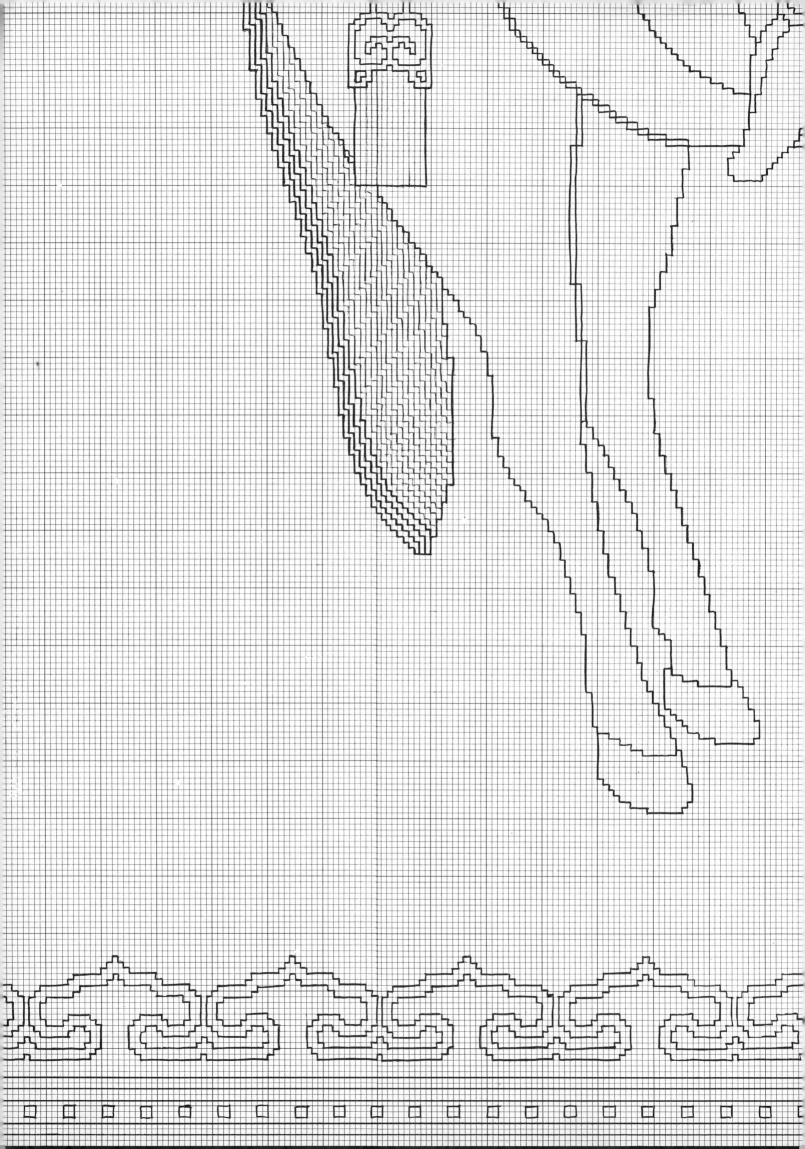

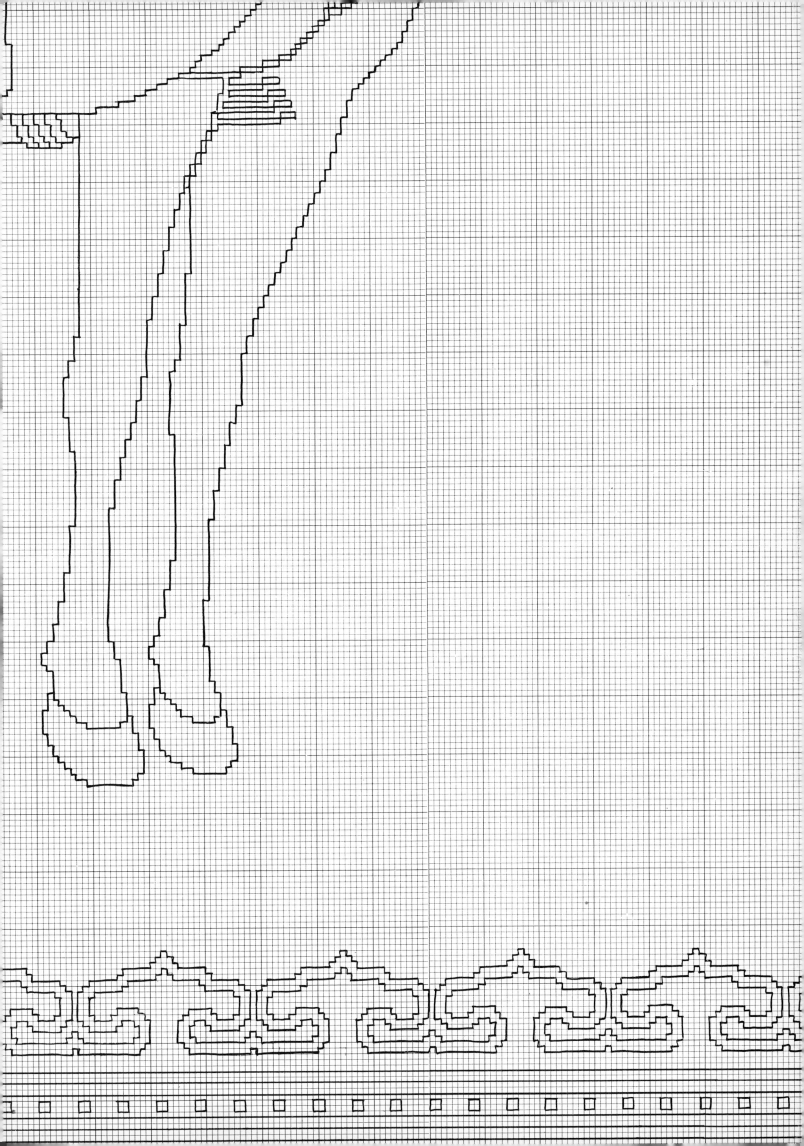

Money II Rug

37" x 75"

Worked on #8 Penelope canvas

The field of this design was adapted from an antique Chinese rug in the collection of the Metropolitan Museum of Art. The border is an adaptation of another antique rug.

The graph thread count is 290 x 586. Bind a piece of #8 Penelope canvas measuring 44" x 82". Mark the horizontal and vertical center lines, and outline the entire work area. Graph lines are not essential in this rug. I suggest instead that you outline the border bands, from the outer edge to the field. Then, counting carefully, outline squares for the coins in the field. Do the same for the coins in the border, and outline rectangles for the Shou, or longevity, character repeated in the border.

The sample rug was made with Persian wool, using the full thread, all three strands. If you want a rug with a tight weave, add one extra strand of wool to the three-strand thread. You will then be working with four strands.

Four tones and colors were used in the Money II rug. The key follows:

017 Off-white	1½ lbs.
382 Light blue	½ lb.
314 Dark blue	½ lb.
136 Tan	2½ lbs.

The sample rug was worked in basketweave by Lois Cowles.

Deer and Crane Rug

35" x 77"

Worked on #8 Penelope canvas

This design was adapted from an antique Chinese rug, plate 7 in *Tapis Anciens de la Chine* by Henri Ernst, Editeur, Paris, France. (M. Ph. Berthelot is the owner of the rug.)

The graph thread count is 282 x 618. Bind a piece of #8 Penelope canvas measuring 42" x 74". Mark the horizontal and vertical center lines. Outline the entire work area. Mark the graph lines in the field of the rug.

The sample rug was made with Persian wool, using the full thread, all three strands. If you want a rug with a tight weave, add one extra strand of wool to the three-strand thread. You will then be working with four strands.

Eight tones and colors were used in the Deer and Crane rug. The key follows:

496 Cream	2¼ lbs.
492 Wheat	¼ lb.
466 Tan	½ lb.
145 Dark tan	¼ lb.
382 Light blue	½ lb.
381 Medium blue	½ lb.
314 Dark blue	1 lb.
424 Orange	¼ lb.

The graph is to be used for both ends of the rug. Work one half of the field, using the color illustration as a guide. Then turn the rug around and work the other half of the field. Fill in the background of the field. Then work the border bands.

The sample rug was worked by Maggie Lane and Louise de Paoli.

Maze and Fretwork Rug

50" x 77"

Worked on #8 Penelope canvas

The elements in this design were taken from several sources. The maze in the center of the rug is a copy of a labyrinth, since destroyed, that once decorated the inlaid marble pavement of the Cathedral of Amiens, built in the thirteenth century. Needless to say, there was no Yang and Yin in the middle of the original design; they are my addition. The corner fretworks were taken from an antique Mongolian rug, then changed a bit. The fretwork pattern that covers the field was found on a Chinese bronze urn of the Han dynasty. The wide border, decorated with repeats of the Yang-and-Yin symbol and the Shou character, for longevity, resembles the borders of a certain type of antique Chinese rug.

The graph thread count is 400 x 620. Bind a piece of #8 Penelope canvas measuring 60" x 74". Mark the horizontal and vertical center lines, and outline the entire work area. Mark the graph lines for the maze and the corner frets. You will not need them for the rest of the design. Instead, outline the border bands, and then outline the areas for the border Yang-and-Yin symbol repeats, and for the character repeats.

The sample rug was made with Persian wool using the full thread, all three strands of it. If you want a rug with a tight weave, add one extra strand of wool to the three-strand thread. You will then be working with four strands.

Three tones and colors were used in the Maze and Fretwork rug. The key follows:

168 Stone gray	1¼ lbs.
145 Nutmeg brown	2¼ lbs.
305 Black navy	2¾ lbs.

NOTE   The rug has an even thread count. However, the fretwork in the field needs an odd thread count. It will therefore be off center by one horizontal and one vertical thread.

The sample rug was worked in basketweave (page 136) by Robert G. Taylor.

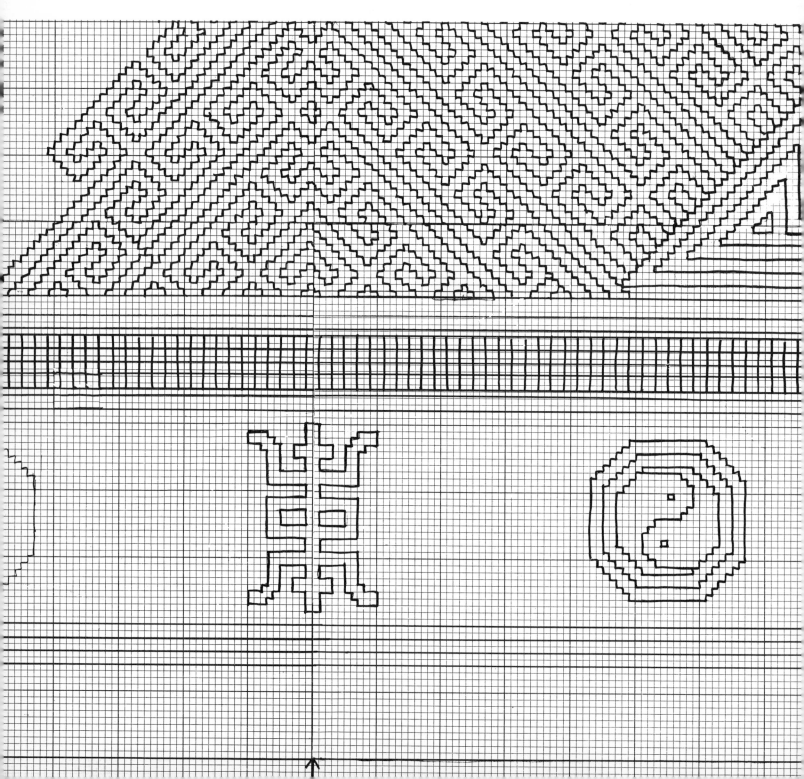

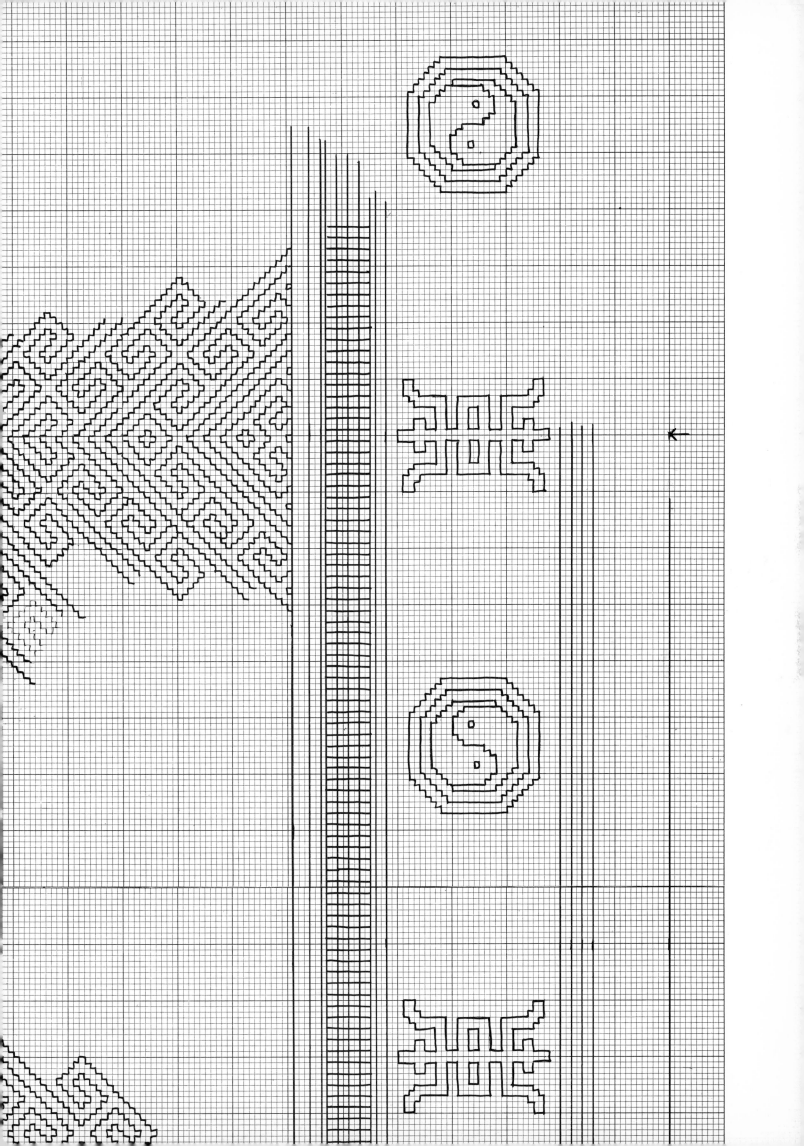

Regal Eagle Hanging Scroll

16½" x 41½"

Worked on #12 mono canvas

This design was adapted from an eagle appearing on a Byzantine silk serge chasuble. I added a halo of thirteen stars and mounted the ensuing combination as a Chinese scroll in order to give us an Oriental commemoration of the American Bicentennial.

The graph thread count is 180 x 485. Bind a piece of #12 mono canvas measuring 22" x 48". Outline the entire work area. Mark the graph lines within the rectangle where the eagle, the upper and lower waves, and the white border will be stitched.

The sample hanging was made with Persian and Medici wool, using two strands of the Persian for the basketweave, and either one or two strands for the other stitches, depending on the effect desired; and using four strands of Medici for the basketweave, and six strands of Medici for the brick stitch in the background.

Three tones and colors were used in the Regal Eagle hanging scroll. The key follows:

104 Rust (Medici wool)	2 skeins
005 White (Paternayan Persian wool)	¼ lb.
382 Blue (Paternayan Persian wool)	½ lb.

The following stitches were used in the Regal Eagle hanging scroll:

1. French Damask stitch with cross-stitch filler used for the outer frame, worked in blue. (page 154)
2. Eyelet stitch used in the white border around the pictorial area. (page 160)
3. Brick stitch used in the background around the eagle. (page 158)
4. French stitch, single, over four and tied over two used in the eagle's neck. Use a single strand. (page 139)
5. Checquer stitch used in the top of the eagle's wing. Use a single strand. (page 150)
6. Smyrna cross stitch in the necklace around the eagle's neck and across the eagle's wings. (page 139)
7. Plaited herringbone stitch in the lower part of the eagle's wings worked between vertical rows of continental stitch. (page 159)
8. Buttonhole half moons for eagle's body and tail feathers. Use a single strand of thread. (page 160)
9. Smyrna cross stitch for the eagle's thighs. Use a single strand of blue for the diagonal cross stitches underneath, then use a single strand of white for the vertical and horizontal cross stitches worked on top of blue stitches. Stagger the horizontal rows of cross stitches for the effect shown in the finished sample. (page 139)
10. Plaited herringbone stitch for the eagle's legs. (page 159)
11. Smyrna cross stitches in the eagle's feet. (see page 139)
12. Ribbed wheels in stars over the eagle's head. Use a single strand of thread for working the eyelet, and also for binding the spokes of the wheels. (pages 138 and 160)

The sample hanging was worked by Maggie Lane.

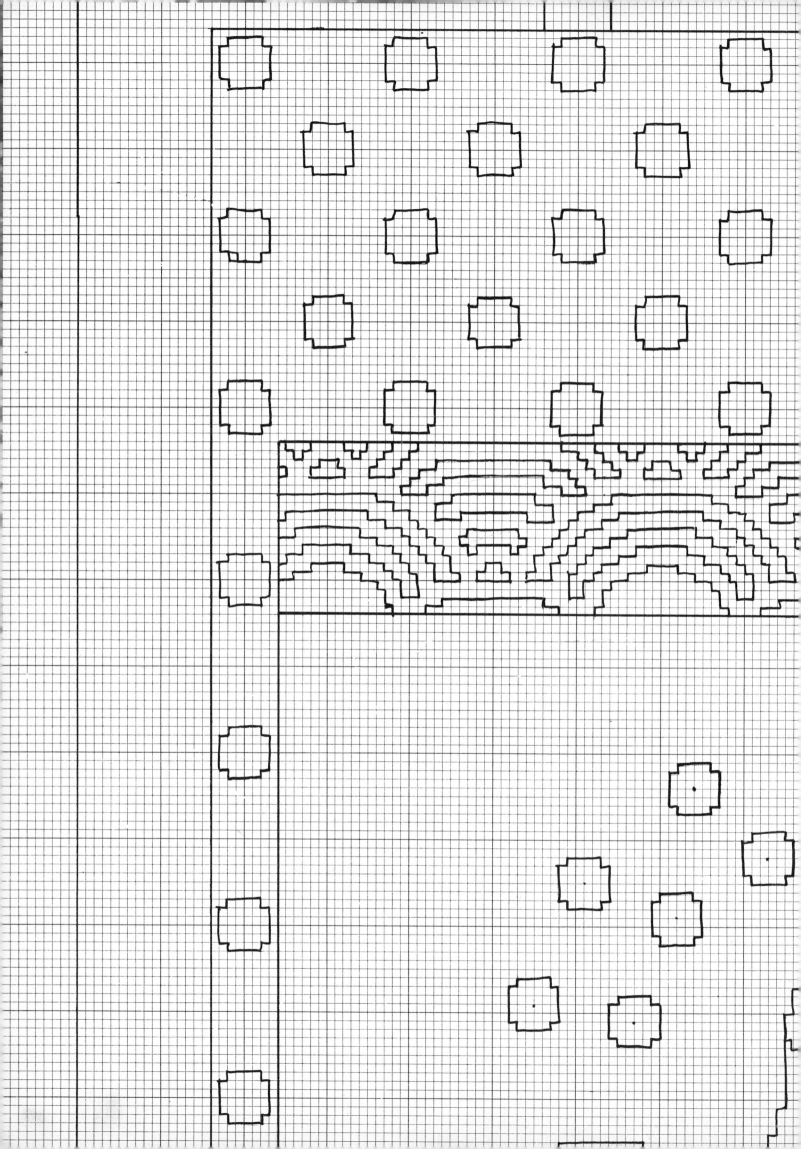

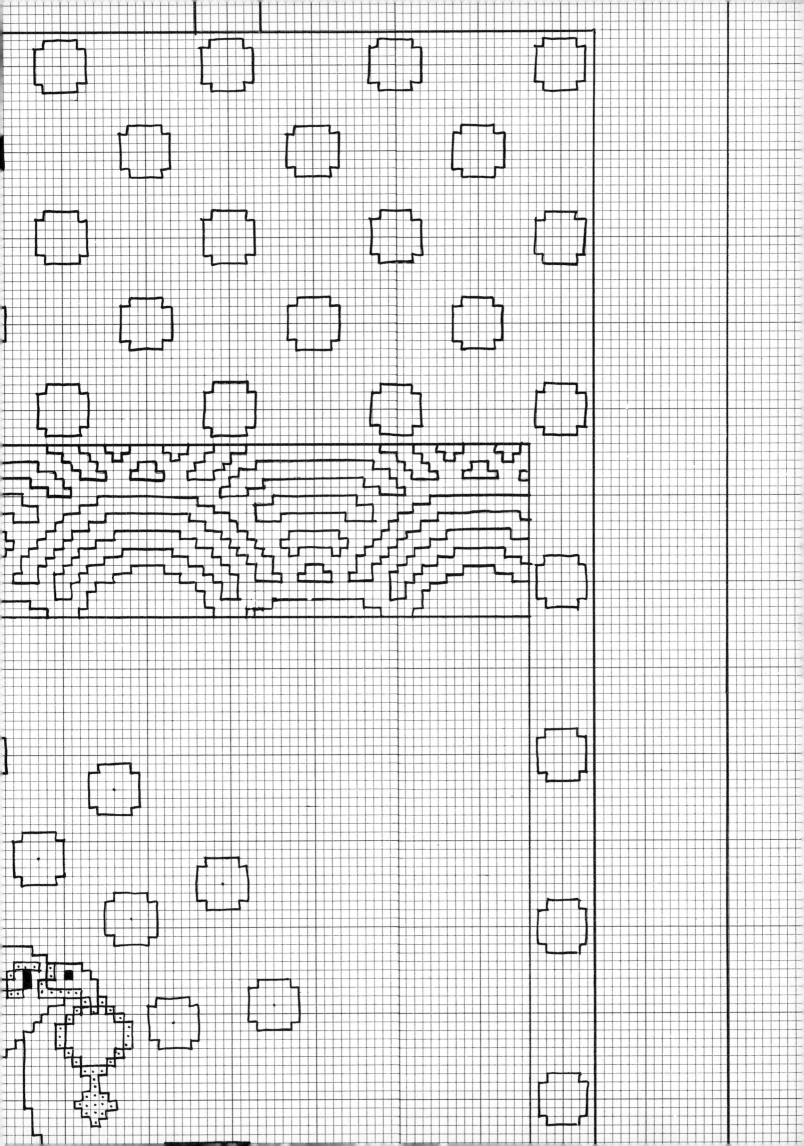

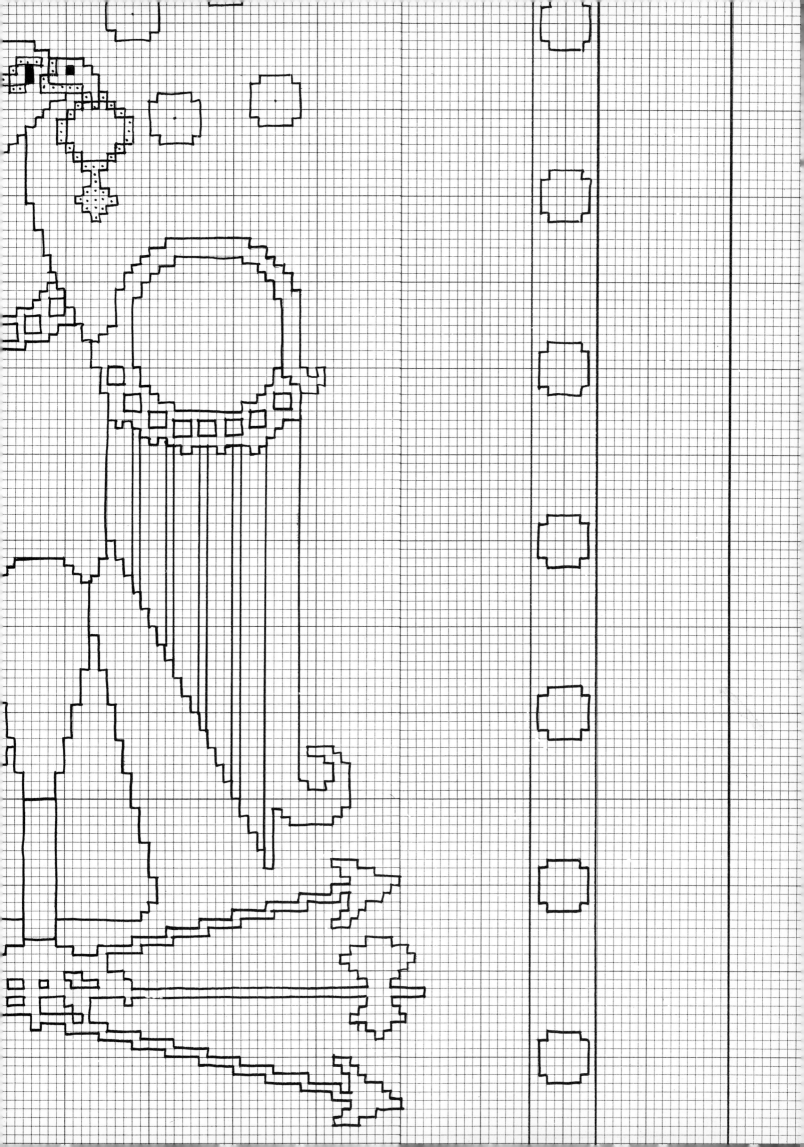

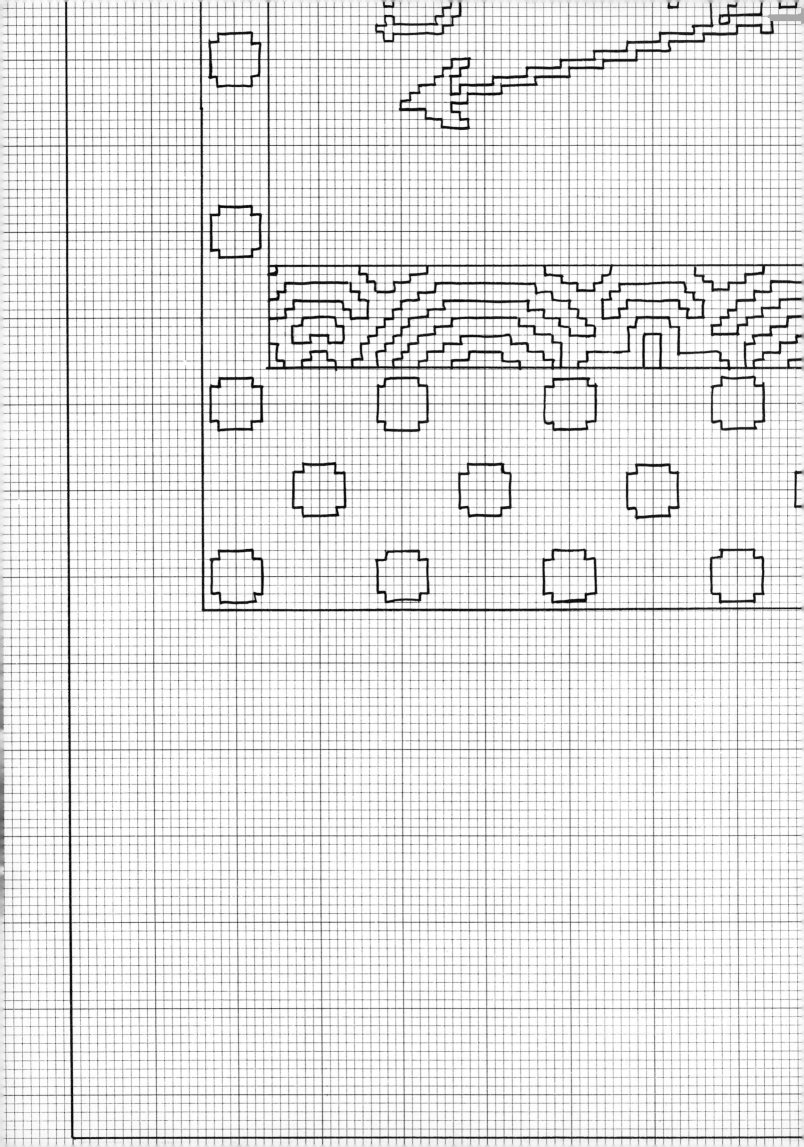

Some Suggestions for Changes That Can Easily Be Made in the Designs in This Book

The Geometric rug can be made longer by adding lozenges and patterned spaces. There are plenty of repeat patterns in this book to allow for a long, long rug. (And *Chinese Rugs Designed for Needlepoint*, Scribners, 1975, offers many more.) Of course, if this rug is worked on #8 Penelope canvas it will automatically become longer and wider than the sample rug. The field of the Geometric rug can be worked in any of the large repeat patterns in this book, and you can change the colors of the rug to suit the color scheme in your home.

The Sacred Mountain rug can be enlarged by working it on #8 Penelope canvas. The colors can be changed, and the repeat pattern in the field can be eliminated or you can use one of the other repeat patterns. In order to lengthen the rug you would need more objects on the side borders. (You can find examples in the Fabulous Border rug in this book's predecessor.)

The Eternal Knot rug would be handsome worked on #8 Penelope canvas. However, the rug should then be worked in the basketweave. The background *could* be worked in the brick stitch, but *never* in the Irish stitch, which on such a large mesh would offer threads so long that they could easily be snagged. The rug can easily be lengthened by the addition of as many sets of eternal knots as you need to achieve the desired length. Color changes in this rug should present no problem whatsoever.

Your ingenuity will surely suggest to you many more possibilities than I have listed here. If you already own *Chinese Rugs Designed for Needlepoint* you would be able to change even the wall hangings, substituting the upper and lower parts of the Elephant panel for the upper and lower parts of the Mongolian archer—or for those used in the Camel and Rider hanging. (In this case, in working the tassels and waves, it would be wise to use only the four tones and colors used in the main body of the Camel and Rider design.)

This book presents a modular system like a set of building blocks. *Chinese Rugs* offers a different set of blocks, like an addition of words to a vocabulary based, however, on the same modular system. I hope that you will find the book now in your hands a pleasure to use, and that with it alone, or in conjunction with my first rug book, you will enjoy making unique and personal works of needlepoint.

The retail mail-order source I recommend for all canvases and wools listed in this book is:

BOUTIQUE MARGOT
26 West 54th Street
New York, New York 10019

The Stitches

Each of the following diagrams has numbered stitches. The numbered end of each stitch is the end where your needle comes up and the stitch begins. The unnumbered end of the same stitch is where your needle goes down and the stitch ends.

CONTINENTAL STITCH

For single-row outlining *only*. If this stitch is used as a background stitch, it distorts the canvas severely.

BASKETWEAVE STITCH

Work in diagonal rows, as numbered in the diagram.

136

IRISH STITCH

Used in the background of the Eternal Knot rug. Also used in the background of the central part of the Camel and Rider panel.

DOUBLE LEVIATHAN STITCH

Used in the camel's tail in the Camel and Rider panel.

SPOKES of RIBBED WHEEL
as used in Camel's Harness in Camel and Rider Panel

Bring whipping thread up through a hole next to the center hole. Whip the wheel spokes as shown in the simplified diagram. Continue whipping until the wheel spokes are covered from the center of the wheel to the edge of the wheel. This may require a second whipping thread after the first thread has whipped as many spokes as it can. Tuck under and secure the remaining end of the first thread. Secure the tail end of the second thread before bringing the second thread up through the canvas where the first thread went under. Continue whipping until the wheel spokes are tightly bound.

RIBBED WHEEL
(simplified to illustrate method of whipping wheel spokes)

SMYRNA CROSS STITCH

Used in the camel's body in the Camel and Rider panel and across the lower edge of the Dragon and Butterflies panel. Also for Lichee Nut #16. Also used in the Regal Eagle hanging scroll for the eagle's legs, and for the dots in his necklace and across his wings. Work in horizontal or diagonal rows.

FRENCH DOUBLE-TIED STITCH

Used in taupe areas of camel's body in the Camel and Rider panel. Also used in the Regal Eagle hanging scroll for the eagle's neck feathers. Work in diagonal rows. Use thinner thread than for regular stitching. Do each vertical stitch twice and each horizontal tie-down stitch once. Pull the yarn when working to enlarge the openings in the canvas. This creates an interesting porous texture.

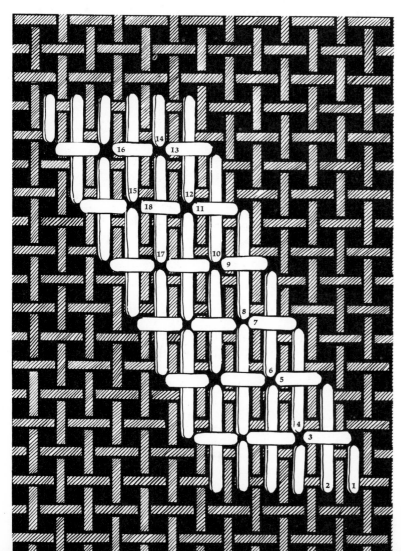

FLAT STITCH

(Medieval German whitework pattern)
Used for taupe areas at the top and bottom
of the Camel and Rider panel. Also used
in the Lichee Nut panel for the #12 lichee
nut. However, in the lichee nut, the Smyrna
cross stitch is used in place of the small
brick-stitch diamonds seen in the diagram.

Work in diagonal rows. When working from

upper right to lower left, you cover more
ground than when you work from the lower
left back up to the upper right. To avoid
confusion I have placed a dot after each
number in the uphill sequence of stitches.
After filling the desired area with the
pattern of stitches as numbered on the
diagram, fill the remaining empty diamonds
with the brick stitch.

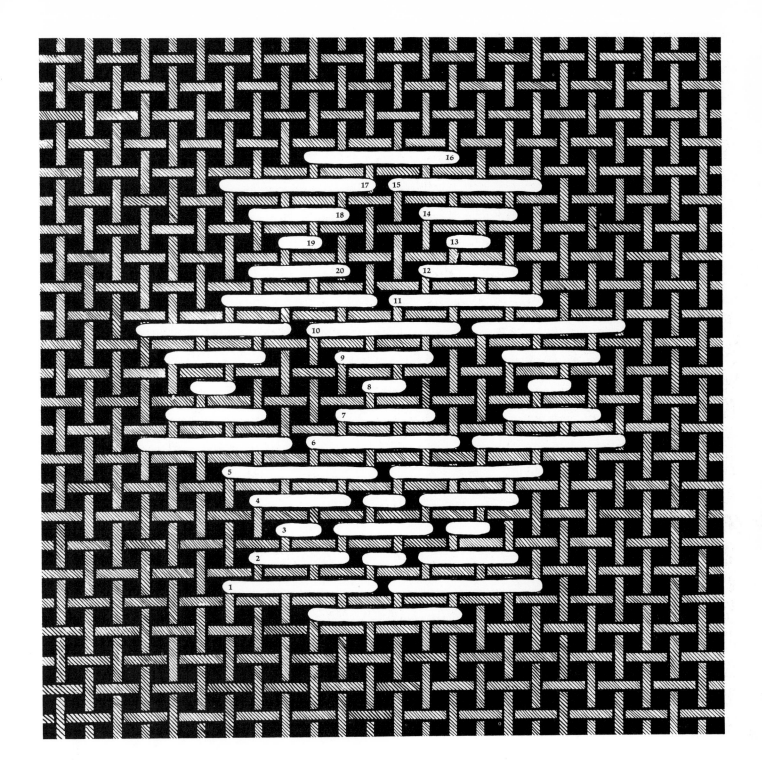

FLAT STITCH

Used in the Lichee Nut panel for the #1 lichee nut. Work in diagonal rows. Turn the canvas at the end of each row so you are always working uphill to the right. Fill the remaining empty diamonds with flat stitch —over two, over four, over two—as shown at bottom of the diagram.

141

STEEPLED SHEAF STITCH

Used in the Lichee Nut panel for the #2 lichee nut. Work this stitch in horizontal rows. Lay vertical flat stitches over four, six, eight, six, and four canvas threads, then tie in the middle. The tie stitch is horizontal and goes over two canvas threads.

DIAMOND CROSS STITCH

Used in the Lichee Nut panel for the #3 lichee nut.

RIDGE FILLING   (pulled yarn)

Used in the Lichee Nut panel for the #4 lichee nut. Work in diagonal rows, pulling the yarn after each stitch to create a pattern of holes.

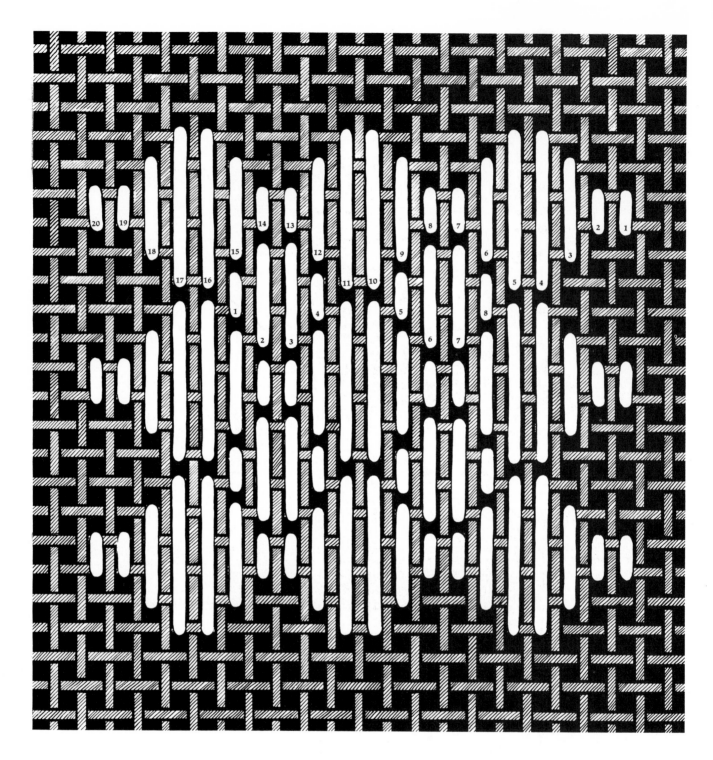

FLAT STITCH

Used in the Lichee Nut panel for the #5
lichee nut.

144

FLAT STITCH with DIAMOND-CROSS FILLER

Used in the Lichee Nut panel for the #6 lichee nut.

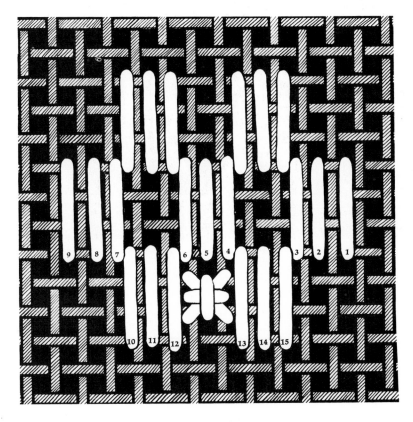

FLAT STITCH with SMYRNA-CROSS-STITCH FILLER

Used in the Lichee Nut panel for the #10 lichee nut.

145

FRAMED CROSS (pulled yarn) with SMYRNA-CROSS-STITCH FILLER

Used in the Lichee Nut panel for the #7 lichee nut. Work horizontal rows of vertical stitches, as numbered. Then work the vertical rows of horizontal stitches, following the same kind of sequence as already used. Fill the empty squares with Smyrna cross stitch.

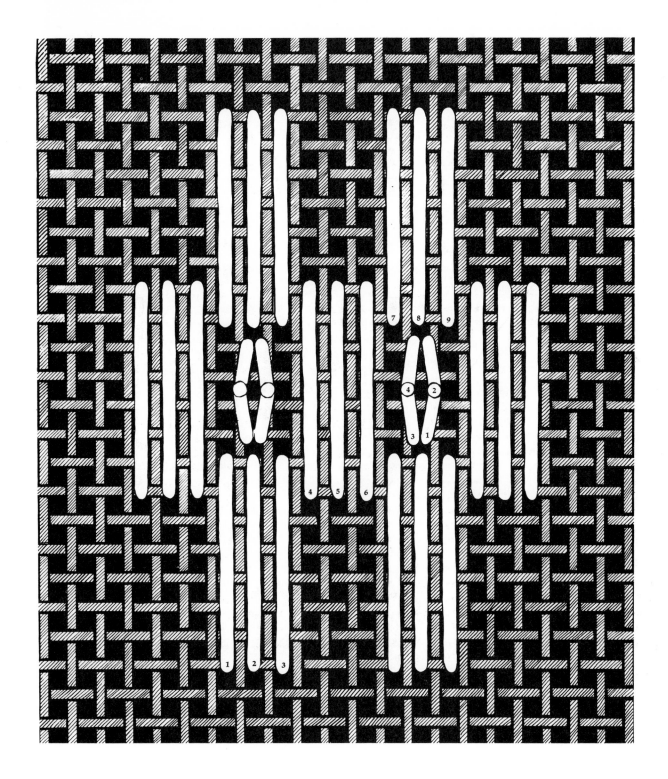

FRENCH DAMASK STITCH with
FRENCH STITCH FILLER

Used in the Lichee Nut panel for the #8
lichee nut.

PATTERNED FLAT STITCH

Used in the Lichee Nut panel for the #9
lichee nut. At the top of the diagram, you
will see the method of constructing the large
tied-down parts of the pattern. Work these
in horizontal or vertical rows. Then fill in
with the flat stitches as numbered in the
diagram.

CASHMERE BLOCKS

Used in the Lichee Nut panel for the #11 lichee nut. Work in horizontal or vertical rows of blocks. Use flat stitch for the #12 lichee nut (see page 140).

FLAT STITCH, STEPPED and TIED

Used in the Lichee Nut panel for the #13 lichee nut.

DIAMOND EYE STITCH (pulled yarn)

Used in the Lichee Nut panel for the #14 lichee nut. Work in diagonal rows, as shown. Work one half of each diamond eye. When the row of half diamond eyes is finished, turn the canvas and work the second half of each diamond eye.

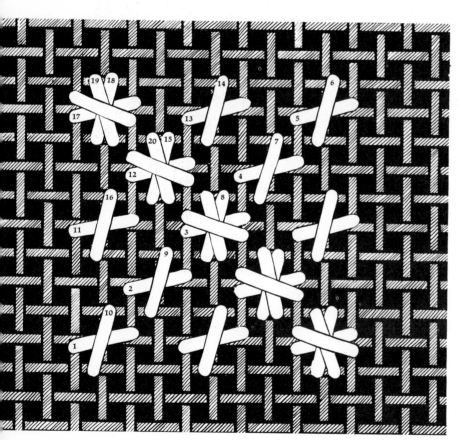

CHECQUER FILLING (pulled yarn)

Used in the Lichee Nut panel for the #19 lichee nut. Also used in the upper part of the Regal Eagle's wings. Work diagonal rows of oblique crosses, working stitches up and down as numbered on the graph. Cover the work area with these crosses slanted, as shown in unfinished stitches. Then turn the canvas 45 degrees. Over the already worked oblique crosses, work the diagonal rows of oblique crosses that will complete each star.

FLAT STITCH with
SMYRNA-CROSS-STITCH FILLER

Used in the Lichee Nut panel for the #17
lichee nut. You can either work the stitches
as numbered or work rows of grouped
horizontal threads, then work the rows of
grouped vertical threads. Work the Smyrna
cross stitches last.

FLAT STITCH with UPRIGHT CROSS FILLER

Used in the Lichee Nut panel for the #15 lichee nut. Work in horizontal or vertical rows of flat stitches. Work upright crosses after all flat stitching has been completed.

152

FLAT STITCH

Used in the Lichee Nut panel for the #18
lichee nut.

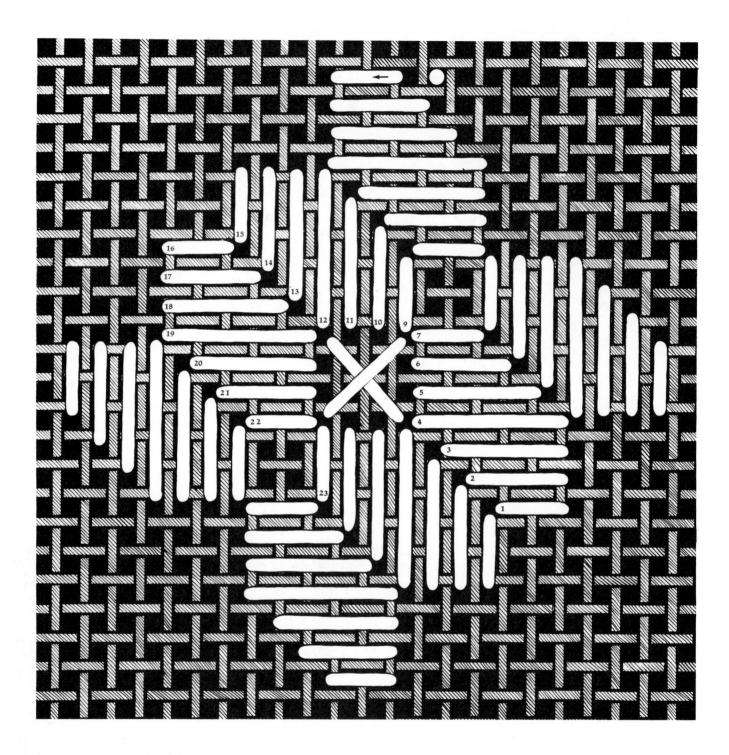

**FRENCH DAMASK STITCH with
CROSS-STITCH FILLER**

Used in the Lichee Nut panel for the #20
lichee nut. Also used in the blue outer
border of the Regal Eagle hanging scroll.

LARGE CROSS STITCH with SMALL UPRIGHT CROSS-STITCH FILLER

Used in the Lichee Nut panel for the #21 lichee nut.

DOUBLE FAGGOT STITCH

(pulled yarn)

Used in dragonfly's wings in the Dragon panel. I have numbered each stitch only once, but work each one twice before going on to the next numbered stitch. Work the first diagonal row. Then turn the canvas upside down and work the second row. Continue in this fashion until you have filled the area you wish to fill.

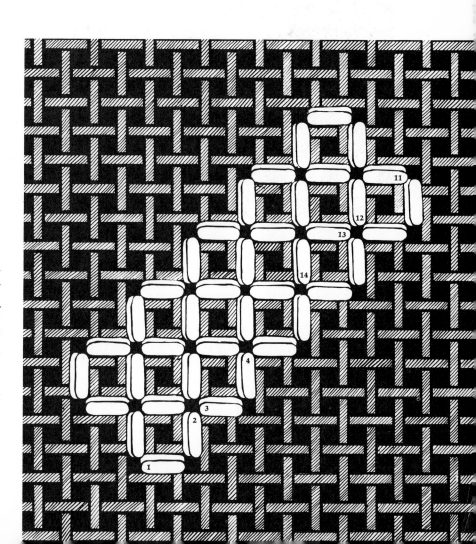

HUNGARIAN STITCH   (worked in
two colors to create a tonal pattern)

Used in the boot of the archer in the
Mongolian Archer panel.

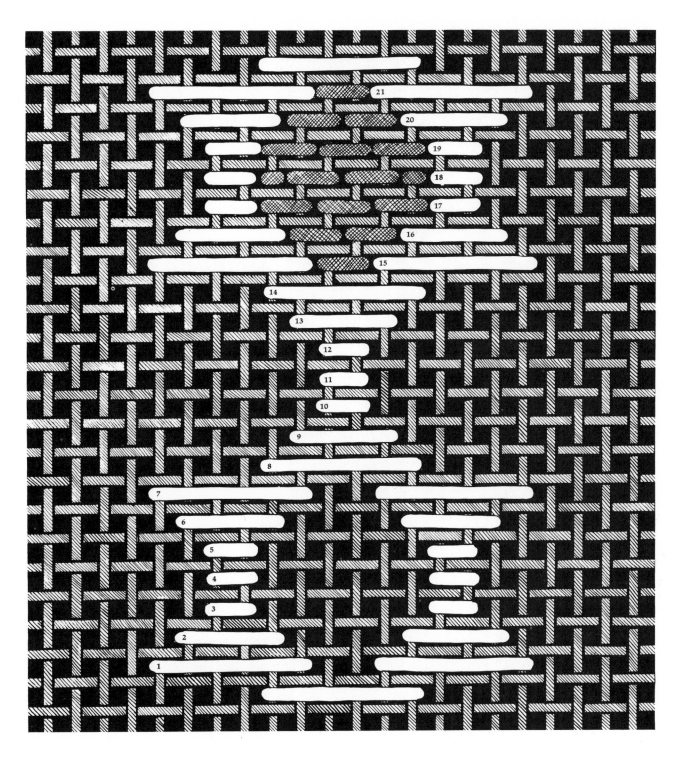

FLAT STITCH   (variation of a fifteenth-century German embroidery pattern)

Used in the pony's saddle in the Mongolian Archer panel.

JACQUARD STITCH

Used in the jacket of the archer in the Mongolian Archer panel.

BRICK STITCH

Used for the background of the center part of the Mongolian Archer panel. Also used in the background around the eagle in the Regal Eagle hanging scroll.

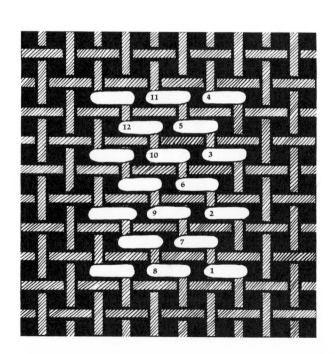

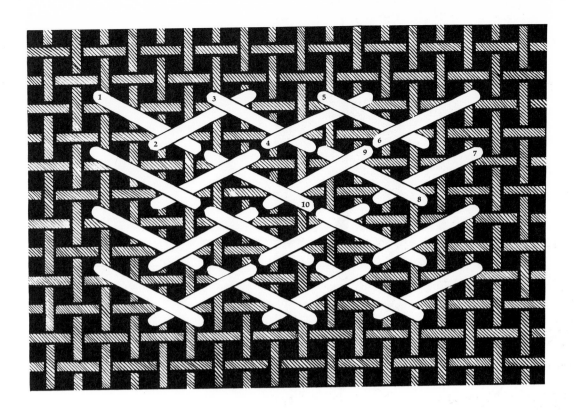

BACK-AND-FORTH HERRINGBONE STITCH

Used for dark-brown areas at the top and bottom of the Mongolian Archer panel. Work from left to right. Turn the canvas upside down, and work, again, from left to right.

PLAITED HERRINGBONE STITCHES

The upper plait, making a braid four canvas threads in width, was used for the Regal Eagle's legs. The lower plait, making a braid three canvas threads in width, was used for the Regal Eagle's blue wing feathers.

BUTTONHOLE HALF MOONS

Used for the Regal Eagle's body and tail feathers. (Turn the canvas upside down to get downward-turning feathers.) Work this stitch in diagonal rows from the lower left to the upper right, as shown on the diagram. As you can see, when you work the buttonhole stitch rather than the half eyelet shown in the first two parts of the diagram, you need a tie-down stitch, the twelfth stitch in the third, upper-right-hand part of the diagram.

For the ribbed wheels and the eyelets in the Regal Eagle hanging scroll, complete the circle, half of which is shown in the first part of the buttonhole-half-moon diagram. Work the full circle around the center hole. There will be sixteen stitches radiating from the center hole.